Studies in Rhetorics and Feminisms

Series Editors, Cheryl Glenn and Shirley Wilson Logan

RETROACTIVISM IN THE LESBIAN ARCHIVES

COMPOSING PASTS AND FUTURES

JEAN BESSETTE

Southern Illinois University Press
Carbondale

Southern Illinois University Press
www.siupress.com

Printed in the United States of America

21 20 19 18 4 3 2 1

Cover illustration: *Beauty Queens* (cropped), copyright © 2013 by David Szauder

Library of Congress Cataloging-in-Publication Data

Names: Bessette, Jean, author.
Title: Retroactivism in the lesbian archives : composing pasts and futures / Jean Bessette.
Description: Carbondale : Southern Illinois University Press, 2018. | Series: Studies in rhetorics and feminisms | Includes bibliographical references and index.
Identifiers: LCCN 2017015538 | ISBN 9780809336234 (pbk. : alk. paper) | ISBN 9780809336241 (e-book)
Subjects: LCSH: Lesbians—United States—Historiography. | Lesbians—Identity—Historiography. | Feminism—United States—Historiography. | Rhetoric—Historiography.
Classification: LCC HQ75.6.U5 B47 2018 | DDC 306.76/630973—dc23 LC record available at https://lccn.loc.gov/2017015538

Printed on recycled paper. ♻

CONTENTS

FIGURES

ACKNOWLEDGMENTS

This book would not exist without Jessica Enoch, whose fusion of intellectual acuity with accessibility and humor has powered me through challenges of many stripes. I am profoundly grateful to Jess for her mentorship, insight, example, and friendship, as well as to Annette Vee, Lester C. Olson, Valerie Rohy, and Steph Ceraso for their support and kindness throughout the process of writing and revising this book. From series editors Cheryl Glenn and Shirley Logan, and an anonymous reviewer, I received insightful and valuable recommendations, which I credit with deepening and refining my arguments. I thank these three for their careful and thoughtful feedback.

Financial support from the University of Pittsburgh and the University of Vermont funded my research trips to the GLBT Historical Society in San Francisco; the Lesbian Herstory Archives in Brooklyn; the June L. Mazer Archives in Los Angeles; and the University of California, Los Angeles, Special Collections. Without this support and these experiences, this project would not be.

Finally, I express my deepest love and gratitude to my partner, Tom, who has been my emotional rock, perceptive reader, and accomplice in adventure. I am so lucky to know him.

Parts of chapter 1 were previously published in my essay “An Archive of Anecdotes: Raising Lesbian Consciousness after the Daughters of Bilitis,” *Rhetoric Society Quarterly* 43.2 (2013): 22–45. Copyright 2013 by the Rhetoric Society of America. Reprinted with permission.

The use of quotations from two folders of correspondence in the Phyllis Lyon and Del Martin Papers is courtesy of the Gay, Lesbian, Bisexual, Transgender Historical Society, San Francisco.

RETROACTIVISM IN THE LESBIAN ARCHIVES

PROLOGUE

> We hope the discussion of lesbian strategies and identities that these objects represent will go on for generations to come, each decade adding its layer of complexity. The fullest record we can leave is the best legacy for the political and social survival of our lesbian daughters around the world. A simplified, homogenized past will not be rich enough in ideas, inspirations, actions, or images to nourish a diverse and embattled lesbian community of the future.
>
> —Joan Nestle, "The Will to Remember"

Broadly conceived, archives have functioned in queer cultures as "a theory of cultural relevance, a construction of collective memory, and a complex record of queer activity" (Halberstam, *In a Queer Time* 169). For lesbian communities in particular, the dynamic functions of cultural relevance, collective memory, and queer activity have made archives more than an inert repository of dead records. Valerie Rohy describes lesbian archives as a "technology of identity," as they have become a medium for tracing past lives in a way that brings "new lives a certain kind of consoling clarity"—by naming, historicizing, and complicating desire's coalescence into enduring sexual identity (354). That "consoling clarity" is needed underscores the presence of competing versions of the past that have shamed and muddled sexual identity with accounts of pathology, crime, and moral deviance.

This understanding of queer archives emphasizes their distinct rhetoricity and the political implications of their creation and interpretation in historiography. For instance, the eclectic array of artifacts contained in New York's Lesbian Herstory Archives (LHA) has consequences beyond the mere preservation of items like the "hard hats and hobnail boots" of lesbian factory workers and the "pasties and glossy prints of a famous lesbian stripper of the fifties" (Nestle, "Will" 1998, 233). LHA cofounder Joan Nestle equates the vast archive of objects to a "discussion of lesbian strategies and identities" ("Will" 1990, 93). She believes the strategies and identities those objects represent could fortify an enduring yet "embattled" sexual identity that is more global, flexible, inclusive, and politic.

This book is a study of how American lesbian collectives like LHA have composed and leveraged the past toward contemporary ends of identification and activism. Inspired by comments like Nestle's, this book emphasizes the rhetorical strategies invented and wielded in the process of composing the past—for, like histories that draw from their contents, the archives examined in this book are indeed *compositions* with implications for lesbian identity and sexual politics. They are crafted for particular audiences in response to historically specific exigencies facing women with same-sex desire. Invigorated by queer challenges to conventional forms of history and archives by scholars such as José Esteban Muñoz ("Ephemera as Evidence") and Ann Cvetkovich (*An Archive of Feelings*), I take an expansive approach to understanding archives and the rhetorical strategies they leverage as a form of *historiography*. Broadly conceived as the collection, arrangement, expression, and even invention of carefully curated "evidence" of the past, queer archives can take unexpected forms and media, ranging from print newsletters and books to material collections of artifacts, from film and digital video archives to ephemeral performances.

After an introductory chapter articulating the rhetorical, historiographic, feminist, and queer theories underpinning this project, the book proceeds through a series of studies of twentieth-century American lesbian collectives who have turned to archives and historiography more broadly in the pursuit of shaping identity and challenging then-present social and political denigrations of same-sex desire and relations.

The introduction traces how rhetorical historiography's disciplinary development, driven by feminist, critical race, and queer critiques, prepares us to turn to historiography in the grassroots. To theorize how composing the past has helped constitute emerging gender and sexual identity, I reconsider Kenneth Burke's notion of rhetoric as identification, emphasizing the role of historiography in the origins of his canonical theory. Connecting Burke's complex theory of identification to the generative rhetorical work of "retroactivism" (a term I've adapted from queer film scholar Lucas Hilderbrand), I argue that rhetors engage in the practice when they compose and appropriate versions of the past toward present identification and politics. This introduction situates *Retroactivism in the Lesbian Archives* in the intersection of feminist and queer rhetorics—thriving disciplinary subfields too often kept distinct—and advocates for increased attention to lesbian rhetors, a population all but ignored in both subfields.

Chapter 1, "The Daughters of Bilitis Archive: Clearing Historical Space for Clustered Anecdotes," focuses on the first lesbian social and political organization in the United States (1955–70). The San Francisco–based national collective strategically deconstructed histories of lesbian pathology in sexology and pulp fiction and replaced them with the experiences of organization members composed in print magazines (the *Ladder*) and books (such as *Lesbian/Woman*). Extending theories of the ephemeral nature of queer archival materials, I argue that these experiences were rhetorically rendered in the form of "anecdotes"; they were then assembled in middle-class categories to challenge associations of lesbianism with pathology and to coalesce a particular lesbian identity characterized by monogamy, femininity, and respectable employment. The inventional effects of this anecdotal rhetorical strategy took the form of "archival consciousness-raising," apparent in the many autobiographical letters the Daughters of Bilitis (DOB) received in response to their print newsletters and books.

Chapter 2, "Classifying Collections: Subversive Schemas as *Topoi* in Place-Based Archives," focuses on two lesbian archives collectives' classificatory procedures for selecting and arranging material artifacts and records. The chapter begins by contextualizing the Lesbian Herstory Archives' and the June L. Mazer Archives' origins and their exigencies, which included the injurious impact of materials in public libraries and official classification systems on women with same-sex desire. In addition to community and educational events, these archives collectives' retroactivism functioned in part by classifying differently than the libraries that had historically closeted queer materials through their procedures of selection, arrangement, and cross-reference. Posing "archivization" as a mode of historical production akin to the DOB's use of alphabetic writing, I frame classification as a rhetorical *topos* and examine its effects on archiving and accessing queer materials. Reconceiving classification as a *topos* accentuates the inextricability of the pattern and the material, and illuminates how archival classification in certain kinds of material space can encourage unanticipated patterns and connections for visitors, creating the conditions for a generative, flexible identity.

Chapter 3, "Remediating the Archive: Documentary Compositions of Lesbian Pasts," examines experimental documentary films produced in the 1990s by filmmakers like Barbara Hammer, Cheryl Dunye, and Jean Carlomusto. These filmmakers employed multimodal rhetorical strategies to frame, refigure, and even invent archival materials in new filmic histories. I suggest that filmic historiographers' retroactivist exigency in the 1990s and early 2000s was in part the rescue or recovery approaches taken by previous generations of retroactivists. The filmic composers sought to nuance the recovery of a glorified lineage of lesbians, because they understood that celebrating individual heroines and sublimating their flaws could cement static, exclusive identifications in the present. They contributed five conceptual innovations to lesbian historiography, each facilitated by a different multimodal rhetorical strategy through which archival media are "remediated" (Bolter and Grusin), remixed, and fabricated.

In each of these chapters, archives are figured in different ways: the founders of the DOB fashioned an archive of anecdotes in their published book, *Lesbian/Woman*; the Lesbian Herstory Archives and the June L. Mazer Archives collectives assembled material collections of artifacts and records; and the contingent of documentary filmmakers reframed and remediated archival materials.

Chapter 4 reflects on the legacy of retroactivism represented by these collectives as a "history of discontinuities" (Vicinus 470): partial, contradictory, yet effective in changing the evidence of the past available for research by women with same-sex desire. This final chapter not only examines how subsequent generations have framed the work of antecedent retroactivists, revealing reverence, remediation, and even affectionate parody in their treatment, but also investigates how retroactivism today reflects and diverges from the strategies, media, and exigencies driving earlier retroactivists. Exploring retroactivism in online new media, I examine the role of digital archivization in lesbian activism and identity formation, focusing on digital video compositions of recent and personal pasts and their implications for the "diverse and embattled lesbian community of the future" that Nestle champions ("Will" 1990, 93).

In drawing together primary sources from newsletters, books, material artifacts and systems of classification, documentary films, and digital video archives, I employ what Halberstam might call a "scavenger methodology": one that

> uses different methods to collect and produce information on subjects who have been deliberately or accidentally excluded from traditional studies of human behavior. The queer methodology attempts to combine methods that are often cast as being at odds with each other and it refuses the academic compulsion toward disciplinary coherence. (*Female Masculinity* 13)

Rather than design my methodology disciplinarily then, I am motivated by driving research questions into the rhetorical mechanisms of retroactivism. While readers may find surprising the move from archives that take the form of books to those that take the form of material collections, documentary films, and digital video assemblages, these primary sources cohere through the understanding that queer and feminist rhetoric will be found in the not-always-conventional media and technologies available to and preferred by disenfranchised collectives. As Elizabeth Freeman explains, queer archives have taken "eclectic, idiosyncratic, and transient" forms, because "sexual dissidents have had to understand what is prior to our own lives with whatever heuristic is at hand" ("Introduction" 162). Seeking historiographic practices where they could be found, I performed research for this book both *in* the Lesbian Herstory Archives (Brooklyn), the June L. Mazer Archives (Los Angeles), and the GLBT Historical Society (San Francisco), and *about* archives like these as ongoing retroactivist projects.

Before I begin my analysis of these collectives' rhetorics of retroactivism, it is important to first step back and reflect briefly on my approach and connections to this project. As a white, middle-class, cisgender woman married to a man, I have, on the face of it, little in common with the gender-transgressive, the visibly queer, the working-class, the nonwhite, and other voices that speak in this book. But this book is precisely about troubling the surface of identity. On the face of it in the midcentury United States, lesbians were understood in terms of mental illness, physical pathology, and irreparable immorality; the association of same-sex desire with enduring sexual identity is a relatively recent phenomenon. This book demonstrates the sheer historiographic *work* rhetors have done since then to transform same-sex desire into a sense of identification with others that belied the individualizing, dispersing effects of discourses of disease and criminality. As a bisexual woman who has rarely felt securely identified with any sexually defined group—usually invisible and passing, surely benefiting from straight, white privilege while losing a sense of belonging regardless of the gender of my partner—I was drawn to these rhetors in admiration of their courage, labor, ingenuity, and resilience in their efforts to form connection and community.

My admiration for these rhetors, however, does not result in a glorification project in the pages that follow. Indeed, my privilege and concealed liminality only enhance my interest in the edges of identification—the individuals who do and do not recognize themselves in compositions of history that purport to trace their pasts. I am invested in denaturalizing the surface of sexual identification, as desire so often exceeds the bounds of presumed straight and gay and, as this book demonstrates, the categories themselves have taken a good deal of rhetorical work to reinforce.

INTRODUCTION
RHETORIC AND IDENTIFICATION IN GRASSROOTS HISTORIOGRAPHY

> Lesbian desire is everywhere, even as it may be nowhere. Put bluntly, we lack any general agreement about what constitutes a lesbian. . . . If we are to make sense of our history, we must look for connections embedded in differences and contradictions.
>
> —Martha Vicinus, "They Wonder to Which Sex I Belong"

There is little consensus on the historical meaning of "lesbian" across time and place, or even within communities. Desire between women is and has always been everywhere, yet the diversity of experiences and the evolution of identity terminology make it impossible to group people and acts in any stable, coherent way. Because we "rarely know precisely what women in the past did with each other in bed or out," historians are unable to "reconstruct fully how and under what circumstances lesbian communities evolved" (Vicinus 434). And yet, however partial and desultory, "histories" of lesbianism have indeed been composed—by the very lesbian communities to which Vicinus refers. Organizations from the Daughters of Bilitis (DOB) to the Lesbian Herstory Archives to contingents of documentary filmmakers have composed versions of a lesbian past, not merely to collect and record the figures, acts, and accomplishments of women with same-sex desire but also to *forge* a sense of shared identity across the time and difference that can divide any group of individuals. Rather than simply reflect an emerging sexual identity, in other words, these historiographic acts actually helped mobilize lesbian identity, to define and coalesce individuals into an abiding sense of collectivity.

Because this sense of collectivity has been hard-earned, fractional, and discontinuous, the subjects in this book traverse "between the queer and the lesbian, not quite occupying either category comfortably" (Cvetkovich,

Archive of Feelings 10). "Queer" has become understood as an orientation against normativity (Jagose, "Trouble with Antinormativity"; Warner, "Introduction"); as I have defined it elsewhere, "someone, or something, is queer when s/he or it challenges the social processes that consolidate and normalize gendered, sexual, raced, and classed identities" (Bessette, "Archive of Anecdotes" 28). Yet describing these collectives and their rhetoric as solely queer fails to acknowledge the ways in which they have coalesced purposively around the identity of lesbian—even as their historiographic rhetoric may redefine what that means and who it marks. "Queer" and "lesbian" sit in tension as terms in this book, always calling attention to the fragility and exclusivity of identities built in the company of others.

This understanding of historiography's implications for forging and disrupting identification contributes new insight into the fields of rhetoric, composition, and communication. While history and historiography have sustained great interest for scholars in these fields since at least the middle of the twentieth century, we have not fully considered the rhetoricity *of* historiography, not only for academic historians but also for the rhetors we study. And yet the evolution of historical scholarship in rhetoric has prepared us well for such an investigation. Since the middle of the century, rhetoric scholars have remained invested in "the rhetorical tradition," writing histories to reclaim forgotten rhetors and rhetorics for our research and teaching. As the decades unfolded into the 1980s and 1990s, historians of rhetoric became particularly concerned with historiography—and with the ideological motivations for and rhetorical consequences of writing history. With attention to gender, race, and class, scholars such as Michelle Ballif, James Berlin, Barbara Biesecker, Cheryl Glenn, Susan Jarratt, Jacqueline Jones Royster, Victor Vitanza, and many others have revised and regendered rhetorical historiography, asking who was being reclaimed by whom and through what methodological principles and assumptions. Because histories of rhetoric emerge from research in archives, interest in the politics of historiography has led to claims about the rhetoricity of archives themselves (Morris, "Archival Turn"; Biesecker, "Of Historicity, Rhetoric"; Sharer, "Disintegrating Bodies") and a proliferation of books interrogating archival research methodology. However, while historiography remains a relevant and robust avenue for scholarly inquiry, the vibrancy and fervor of this interest has mainly been contained to the theorization of our own scholarly positions, methods, and exigencies as academic historians.

Turning attention to the role of historiography in the grass roots, *Retroactivism in the Lesbian Archives* extends discussions of the rhetorical, ideological, and gendering work of historiography into new arenas by locating activist historiographers outside the university. Grassroots historiography and its role in shaping identification are always also political, involving the invention of strategies of self-definition that speak not only to women with same-sex desire but also to competing associations of lesbianism with moral, criminal, and psychological deviance.

Consider the strategy behind the naming of the DOB, the first American lesbian organization, founded in 1954. The figure of Bilitis first appeared in late nineteenth-century France when a man named Pierre Louÿs claimed to unearth a lost book of her poems. Louÿs contended that Bilitis was a fatherless student of Sappho's, raised under her tutelage on the isle of Lesbos in Greek antiquity. While Sappho was well known in Victorian times for her legacy as a teacher and her love poems for other women, her own extant lyrics stopped short of describing same-sex intimacy. But Bilitis's poems were explicit in their erotic descriptions, "implicating Sappho in a homosexual scenario far more graphic than anything contained in her [own] poetry" (Dejean 278). Bilitis's poetry seemed to confirm and even invent a "sexualized Sapphic pedagogy" (Dejean 278), infusing Sappho's memory as a teacher of girls with myths of her seduction of innocent students like Bilitis.

While Bilitis's historical association with female same-sex desire might make her seem an appropriate choice as a foremother to a lesbian organization, she was revealed to be a hoax not long after Louÿs's "discovery" was made public. As it turned out, he had invented her name and poetry whole cloth, hoping to find notoriety and legitimacy in her ancient Greek provenance. Bilitis, a fictional woman fabricated by a French man, should seem an odd namesake for the American lesbian collective after all. Why might a twentieth-century women's activist organization position itself as the progeny of a nineteenth-century man's lie?

Rather than reveal the DOB's ignorance of her fraudulent origins, the collective's appropriation of Bilitis instead demonstrates the role of historiography—in this case, the strategic construction of lineage—in their formation of identification. The figure of Bilitis functioned for the organization in two ways: through her enigma and her associations with culturally revered epochs and institutions. Because Bilitis was not in the realm of popular knowledge in midcentury American culture, the organization of women could claim they were merely a poetry club if pressed to explain her, helping the collective to negotiate censorship and repression. Bilitis's enigma was *useful* in the era of McCarthy, when even the suspicion of homosexuality could be grounds for arrest and harassment. But her mystery also made her malleable; she could be fashioned differently for different audiences. The organization's name deflected attention from its focus on sexuality with its nominal connotations of longstanding patriotic women's service institutions like the Daughters of the American Revolution, as the acronym "DOB" could be seen to resonate with and even echo the much-revered DAR. Additionally, Bilitis's "origins" in an esteemed Greek epoch garnered regard for the group whose members positioned themselves as her progeny. These associations lent legitimacy and *legacy* to an organization whose very purpose was considered illegitimate, pathological, and even criminal. The collective's choice of a name begins to suggest the kind of lesbian identity they sought to shape, characterized by middle-class values of femininity, respectability, and other bastions of social conformance.

Any discussion of Bilitis cannot be about "what was," because she never was, but it can be about how and why she was employed rhetorically in a lineage of constructed history that exposes the politics of shaping identity. As the appropriation of Bilitis suggests, the rhetorical composition of history does not take place in a void but instead intervenes in existing accounts to create contemporary change or stasis. The collectives examined in this book were faced with accounts of lesbianism that were not of their own making: sexological studies that claimed physical pathology, psychological studies that diagnosed mental illness, fictional accounts that punished immorality. The displacement—and replacing—of pejorative accounts of lesbianism with new versions of the past is an activist strategy to effect change in the present and, as Michel de Certeau maintains, "a fashion of *making a place for the future*" (85, his emphasis). This, I argue, is retroactivism.

Here "retroactivism" is adapted from Hilderbrand, who coined the term to describe the role of "imagining, feeling, and drawing from history" (308) in his own present "political and sexual identity formations" (303). For Hilderbrand, his nostalgia for the late 1980s through the early 1990s prime of the radical queer activist group ACT-UP (AIDS Coalition to Unleash Power) is generative. Though he admits that he idealizes his memories of the group despite the centrality of trauma and loss in AIDS activism, the past he remembers is a fusion of queer politics with "polymorphous desire" and "subversive sensibilities" (Hilderbrand 305) that inspires his present work toward a queerer future. For Hilderbrand, retroactivism is the generative function of shaping and drawing from the past for present identity formation and future politics.

My extension of the term acknowledges Hilderbrand's definition of retroactivism but also recognizes that such generative work often requires more than nostalgia. In this study, retroactivism manifests as lesbian collectives impugn, deconstruct, and scavenge existing historical accounts and libraries, and compose new histories and archives out of the detritus to shape identification and political leverage. Each of the collectives I examine have recognized that one way to rhetorically combat political harassment, shame, and isolation is to revisit historical narratives that naturalize present characterizations of lesbians as mentally, physically, and morally aberrant. They then co-opt, challenge, modify, and replace these versions of the past with complex, experiential, and queer compositions.

Lesbian rhetors' turn to retroactivism is not surprising, for historiography has long been endemic in queer cultures and studies. Because "gays and lesbians have been figured as having no past: no childhood, no origin or precedent in nature, no family traditions or legends, and crucially, no history as a distinct people" (Freeman, "Introduction" 162), fulfilling a voided past holds special significance in queer discursive practices. As Scott Bravmann maintains, historiography has performed a number of functions against this backdrop of historical amnesia, serving to "foster community, expand public and private discourses on sexuality, [and] construct queer subjectivity" (Bravmann 45). Collecting, composing, and revising the past is not unique to queer cultures, of course, but it has been an important mode of activism and identity building in the twentieth century.

Representatively, in the introduction to their anthology of gay and lesbian recovery projects, Martin Duberman, Vicinus, and George Chauncey argue that "some of the most important issues facing, agitating, and sometimes dividing" lesbian and gay communities "today, personally and collectively, are *best addressed historically*" (11, my emphasis). Because their history has been neglected or elided in institutionalized documentation, lesbian and gay people's

> hunger for knowledge of their past is strong. Having struggled to create a public presence for themselves in the world today, they seek to reclaim their historical presence. For many, gay history helps constitute the gay community by giving it a tradition, helps women

> and men validate and understand who they are by showing them who they have been. (Duberman et al. 12)

The insistent engagement with the past in queer cultures and studies emerges from the pervasive sense that enduring traumas can be redressed through a rescue of and return to the scenes of historical injury—and, further, that sexually identified communities can be legitimated and reinforced through the development of a shared sense of the past.

This preoccupation with the past's relationship to present sexual identity has meant that temporality, historicism, and the archive have remained a principal focus in interdisciplinary queer studies for almost two decades, evidenced by the influential work of literary, performance, and media scholars such as Bravmann, Cvetkovich, Carolyn Dinshaw, Halberstam (*Female Masculinity*, *In a Queer Time and Place*), Freeman (*Time Binds*), Heather Love, Muñoz ("Ephemera"), and Christopher Nealon among many others. Nealon, for instance, investigated how queer texts from the twentieth century illuminated "an overwhelming desire to *feel historical*, to convert the harrowing privacy" of pathology into "some more encompassing narrative of collective life" (8, his emphasis). Cvetkovich's groundbreaking work *An Archive of Feeling* argued that this emergent collective life—what she calls "lesbian public cultures"—was produced out of the trauma and resilience represented in a diverse archive, ranging across oral histories, literature, film, and performance.

Building on the foundation laid by these scholars, this book's focus on the *rhetorical* dimensions of queer/lesbian archives as a form of historiography marks its contribution to queer studies more broadly. For instance, Bravmann argues that images of the gay and lesbian past "animate the present" in an ongoing "hermeneutic and political struggle in the formation of new social subjects and new cultural possibilities" (4). However, while Bravmann understands that these representations of the past are "dynamic rhetorical performances" (4), he does not attend to the specific rhetorical strategies employed by queer communities as they cohere and contest identification.[1] And yet historiography in general and, as Morris argues, archives in particular "function ideologically and politically" ("Archival Queer" 146). While rhetorical scholars, including Rawson, Alexander and Rhodes, and Cram, have taken up Morris's charge in diverse and innovative ways, this project is among the first book-length treatment of the subject and the only to focus on queer/lesbian rhetors.

RHETORIC AND IDENTIFICATION IN RETROACTIVISM

When collective rhetors such as the DOB, the Lesbian Herstory Archives, and filmic historiographers engaged in historiography that helped cohere provisional gender and sexual identities, they unknowingly contributed to a simultaneously evolving conversation about the relationship between rhetoric and identification. While classical perspectives defined rhetoric as the art of persuasion in formal legal, political, and religious speech, Burke's alternate definition from his 1950 *Rhetoric of Motives* more productively illuminates the role of rhetoric in the formation of collective identity. Burke argues that the motivations for rhetorical activity are primarily directed toward the establishment of shared investments (or the perception of them), which Burke calls "identification." The establishment of shared investments through rhetorical acts then forms a foundation for collective identity, for as Diane Davis argues in her description of Burke, "there can be no identity without identification, and there can be no identification without the suasive force of meaningful figures" (127).

When Burke first explained his theory in *A Rhetoric of Motives*, he invoked the connection between identification and historiography I have described. Detailing the example of a poet who identifies with a fallen, holy hero in his retelling, Burke describes the "uses" of a "ritualistic *kind of historiography* in which the poet could, by allusion to a Biblical story, 'substantially' foretell the triumph of his vanquished faction" (*Rhetoric* 19, my emphasis). For Burke, John Milton's identification with Samson (with his blindness, his fall, his tragic victory) was a rhetorical move, a way of defining and elevating the poet through association with a heroic figure who died in a noble cause: killing the Philistines who blinded him, and killing himself in the process. While Burke's association of rhetoric and identification has become canonical in rhetorical studies, his emphasis on the role of *historical* appropriation in this process—a turning to the past—has been largely overlooked.[2]

I point to this famous Burkean example with awareness of its vexed position in a feminist and queer context such as this book. As Kyle Jensen and Krista Ratcliffe argue, Burke's historical or "mythic" examples often depend on a woman's negation through the "deceitful woman trope": here, Samson's lover Delilah, who discovered and destroyed the hirsute source of his strength in exchange for eleven hundred silver shekels. Though Milton's poem belabors Samson's fall at the hands of a "deceitful Woman," that "specious monster" (*Samson Agonistes* 201, 230), Burke homes in on a different motive for Milton's identification: perhaps Milton saw in Samson's tragic victory a religiously sanctioned avenue of suicide, a means of valiant transformation from his lived experience as "an old poet, libertarian and regicide, blind, fallen on evil days" to heroic conqueror of the Philistines' analog, the British Royalists he so opposed (Burke, *Rhetoric* 3).[3] In his reading of Milton's "ritualistic kind of historiography" (19), from which the theory of identification is derived, Burke does not see or name the silent Delilah, who is present only as the plot device that makes possible the decimation of the Philistines-qua-Royalists, the transformation from blind poet to heroic martyr.

How then do we appropriate and extend a rhetorical theory derived from a "historiography" that silences woman? Perhaps the answer comes from Burke himself, who argues that we "need not close our eyes" to the inevitability of faction and conflict in rhetoric and human relations alike; instead we "can be on the alert always to see how such temptations to strife are implicit in the institutions that condition human relations"—here, gender bias—while "*we can at the same time always look beyond this order, to the principle of identification in general*" (*Rhetoric* 20, my emphasis). The principle of identification, as Burke asserted, depends on division, exerts itself in compensation for division, wrestles with division across a "wavering line of pressure and counterpressure" (*Rhetoric* 23). Turning Burke on Burke then, we can harness the concept of rhetoric as identification to investigate the complexity of gender and sexual identity formation itself with particular attention to its inexorable fissures.

Identification between individuals is more complex and "ambiguous" than simple similarity. Burke explains:

> Here are the ambiguities of substance. In being identified with [Person] B, [Person] A is "substantially one" with a person other than himself. Yet at the same time he remains unique, an individual locus of motives. Thus he is both joined and separate, at once a distinct substance and consubstantial with another. (*Rhetoric* 21)

Though individuals may nominally cohere in identification by composing and believing a shared sense of their past, this consubstantiality does not eliminate individual difference between members of each group. As Raymond Williams reminds, "even in the simplest group, there are, as in a 'society,' relations of tension and conflict as well as cooperation" (83).[4]

Consequently, there is always tension between collectivity and difference (this is Burke's "wavering line") and we must take care to illuminate the "edges" or limits of identification: the individuals who both do and do not recognize themselves in the sexual identities the collectives seek to rhetorically shape through historiography.

Despite the enduring influence of Burke's theory of identification, rhetorical critics rarely attend to discursive construction of identity or the complexity of individual difference within identification. As Ralph Smith and Russell Windes argue in their chapter in Morris's *Queering Public Address*, "many rhetorical critics . . . take for granted that collective actors speak automatically from a transparent identity and therefore the only rhetorical decisions are those that concern how a given identity is to be presented to a particular audience" (54). Instead of looking only at how a fully formed identity is *wielded* to an outside audience, this book looks more fully into the complexities of sexual identity formation and narration by attending to their discursive creation and disruption—to the historical and rhetorical forces that shape contests over the definition of specific sexual identities.

Delving deeper into the role of rhetoric in identification, I focus on the granular rhetorical strategies lesbian collectives have employed to construct and leverage certain versions of the past: the inventive *textual, visual, audio, and material* moves and their effects on the collective and more general publics. Rather than pose history grandly as "discourse" and make broad claims for its impact, I investigate the process and product of the rhetorical activity of historical representation. Precisely what strategies did collective rhetors employ, appropriate, or invent to forge a convincing and effective account of the past? How did they persuade women with same-sex desire to adopt and contribute to this collective rhetorical project? Ultimately, to what identity-shaping and political ends was such historiography put in the fight to define the present and future?

Emphasizing the composition and engagement with historiography in the grass roots points to the role of literate activity outside formal schooling in the lives of marginalized groups. Jacqueline Jones Royster defines literacy in such communities as individuals' capacity to access and use information "to articulate lives and experiences and also to identify, think through, refine, and solve problems . . . over time" (*Traces of a Stream* 45). Like Royster's study of African American women's literacy practices, the individuals in this book compose (past) experience to "identify, think through, refine, and solve problems" (45) of identificatory dispersion and political marginalization. Thus the choice between emphasizing "literacy" or "rhêtoric" as a key term is a difficult one. As Brenda Glascott argues, emphasizing rhetoric over literacy has deep implications for what we focus on and value in our research. For Glascott, Royster's focus on literacy practices allows her to emphasize the "process of self-creation" of black women essayists, because literacy as a key term encourages scholars to see "self-directed" language acts in addition to the "other-directed" acts she ascribes to rhetoric: Royster's "essayist uncovers herself to herself as she writes."

As this book suggests, however, these "directions" are rarely independent of one another. The DOB shaped middle-class, socially conforming lesbian identification in part *as* a political move—to challenge dominant stereotypes of lesbians as criminal and deviant—and the "other-directed" retroactivist rhetoric had implications for how members of the DOB understood themselves and their relationship to other lesbians. Posing rhetoric as the key term allows a consistent focus on this complex relationship between identity-shaping and political work as it explicitly draws attention to the uses and effects of strategies of identification.

FEMINIST/QUEER/RHETORICAL HISTORIOGRAPHY

This study of retroactivism relies on a confluence of work by rhetorical scholars who specialize in feminist, queer, and technology areas, as well as broader conversations about queer historiography outside rhetorical studies. *Retroactivism in the Lesbian Archives* demonstrates that, despite their separate subdisciplinary tracks, feminist and queer rhetoric and historiography share a number of fundamental principles. This book sits between these theoretical trajectories, calling attention to where they overlap, diverge, and productively challenge one another.

Like feminist rhetorical scholars such as Glenn, Royster, Jarratt, and many others, I understand that gender bias in our disciplinary history matters because, as Glenn asserts, histories "do (or should do) something" in the present: "choosing what to show and how to represent it . . . subtly shape[s] our perceptions of a rhetoric englobed" ("Remapping" 291). Feminist historiographic scholarship has primarily been directed at the male-dominated rhetorical tradition—the canon of rhetorical history that defines what rhetoric and its best practices are (Enoch, "Releasing

Hold").[5] The absence of women rhetors in this canon functioned as a legitimation of the continuing exclusion of women rhetors. Like retroactivists in this study, feminist historiographers have always been motivated by the understanding that the way we write history has implications for gender politics. And, as a feminist historiographer myself, I understand that it matters in the present how history is written, and that historiography is always gendered, whether it is "traditional" or explicitly feminist.

But, to work through the nuances of my extension and intervention in feminist historiography, it is important to outline in more detail the primary approaches taken by feminist scholars as they challenge traditional rhetorical historiography. Thus far, feminist scholars have carved out two primary methodological tracks in pursuit of their collective challenge to the rhetorical tradition: recovery and gender-analytic "rereading." Recovery projects endeavor to unearth rhetorical women from the dustbins of history, reclaiming them for the disciplinary tradition. This approach has resulted in a spate of important projects rescuing individual women rhetors for our teaching and scholarship and demonstrating their rhetorical significance (for example, Campbell, *Man Cannot Speak for Her*; Lunsford). However, the recovery approach has been critiqued by some feminist historiographers, such as Michelle Ballif ("Re/Dressing") and Biesecker ("Coming to Terms"), for reinforcing the ideological system—exclusive canonization, patriarchal criteria for value and credibility—that produced the need for recovery of women into history in the first place. These scholars thus advanced projects that reread the rhetorical tradition and interrogated the ways historical knowledge was produced and made meaningful through gender. Inspired by feminist historian Joan Scott, Jarratt defined this approach as "gendered analysis" to emphasize how gender is always operative, including in prominent male-authored texts in the dominant tradition ("Speaking" 193).

Yet, even in 1990 when Jarratt wrote to advocate gendered analysis in addition to recovering women rhetors, she cautioned against dividing and ranking these two approaches (195). This book engages both recovery and rereading in an effort to move the conversation in feminist historiography beyond these two longstanding methodologies and the illusion of their mutual exclusivity.[6] Like a recovery project, my studies of lesbian collectives provide proof that women have successfully invented and leveraged strategies for writing and speaking, despite—or more precisely *because*—of their gendered and sexualized positions.[7]

Yet, like proponents of gender-analytic rereading, I also stake out my intervention by questioning the terms of recovery projects: the field's primary focus on heterosexual women. My focus on how collectives have leveraged rhetoric *in order to* cohere in gender and sexual identification unsettles what many feminist historiographers have taken as given: the universal category of "woman," which is almost always implicitly heterosexual. As Rawson contends, recovery projects in feminist historiography have proceeded with an unquestioned reliance on "fixed-identity categories, typically 'woman' or 'female,'" and have most frequently recovered "a gender-normative body of texts—those produced by biologically born, self-identified or historically identified women" (40). And yet rereading approaches have also been complicit in these assumptions. Though rereading projects "engage with oppressive gender roles and stereotypes," they rarely challenge static "gender binaries and logics" (Rawson, "Queering" 40). Rawson points out that he has not encountered a definition of "woman" in these histories and wonders if such omissions reveal the assumption that women "simply are," and thereby risk excluding the diversity of gender and sexual identifications that might exist within, and put pressure on, such categories. Instead of viewing gender and sexuality as certitudes, Rawson invites scholars to take on historical and political projects that understand these identifications as a "complex identity production and performance" (41).

This project engages in a queer critique of feminist historiography's tendency to focus on normatively gendered and implicitly heterosexual women by pursuing a historiographic project that does not take gender and sexuality as given, universal identity categories. Instead I examine how rhetors have composed the past together *in order* to identify as women and as lesbians, often by positioning themselves against other definitions of women and lesbians.

My focus on lesbian retroactivist collectives as rhetors is in part an attempt to complicate feminist historiography's tacit assumption of a normatively gendered and sexually identified rhetor. But I also focus on lesbian collectives, rather than, for example, lesbian *and* gay male collectives as a feminist rereading of some queer studies scholarship that seems to equate homosexuality with white gay men. As Diana Fuss asserts, some gay male historians either "effect a complete and total silence on the subject of lesbianism while implicitly coding homosexuality as male" or "situate lesbianism as a footnote to gay male history—the subordinated other in a newly constructed gay/lesbian binarism" (Fuss 110).[8] In recovering lesbian collectives then, this book is a feminist rhetorical intervention in a historical tendency to "code homosexuality as male" (Fuss 110). Whether one surveyed contributions to feminist or queer rhetorical histories, she would find little emphasis on lesbian or bisexual women rhetors.

Consequently, *Retroactivism in the Lesbian Archives* draws feminist and queer rhetorical work into conversation in the hopes that a nuanced approach to gendered and sexual rhetorics might emerge. Prevalent among recent scholars of queer rhetoric is a growing focus on the symbolic and performative strategies that have constructed queer subjects against normativity. Queer rhetoric is oppositional by definition; Jonathan Alexander and Jacqueline Rhodes define it as the "self-conscious and critical engagement with normative discourses of sexuality in the public sphere that exposes their naturalization and torques them to create different or counter-discourses, giving voice and agency to multiple and complex sexual experiences." Queer rhetoric, in other words, has been defined more by its oppositional tactics vis-à-vis normativity than by the contemporary sexual identity categories of "gay" and "lesbian."

As with queer studies more broadly, queer rhetoricians frequently turn to historiography—to methodology, archives, and media of the past—in our attempts to locate rhetorical practices in both "queer" and "straight" archives. Morris, for example, encourages scholars to be "archival queers": to "utilize the tools of rhetorical criticism and theory to enhance navigation of archives and produce rhetorical histories of archives that will warrant and arm our queer scholarship, pedagogy, and activism" ("Archival Queer" 147). Morris is advocating a queer orientation *toward* archives: a critical, rhetorical analytic that examines how archives produce and encourage normativity or queerness. Advancing the inroads recently made by these scholars, I investigate the rhetorical strategies that lesbian-identified collectives have employed to compose and leverage archives and histories as an activist move against normalizing discourses.

However, this book is also a caution against the exclusions that even queer rhetorical scholarship can precipitate. The collectives I study are queer by Alexander and Rhodes's definition only to varying degrees. For Alexander and Rhodes, "queer rhetoric is certainly concerned with lesbian, gay, bisexual, and transgender (LGBT) issues, identities, and politics, but it is not exclusively linked to them and may in fact resist certain kinds of gay and lesbian normalization." Were this project defined solely by a focus on queerness as an orientation against prefigured notions of normativity, the DOB might once again be erased from rhetorical history, for this lesbian collective would likely be considered conservative and assimilationist by contemporary queer critics: too normative to be queer. Lisa Duggan, for example, might describe the collective as "homonormative," as the DOB enacted a politics that "does not contest dominant heteronormative assumptions and institutions but upholds and sustains them" (*Twilight of Equality* 50). For Duggan and other queer critics, the danger of homonormativity is a "demobilized gay constituency" that is "depoliticized" and "anchored in domesticity and consumption" (50).

Thus, one intervention I make in queer rhetorical studies is the recuperation of lesbian rhetorical activity that fails to meet contemporary standards for queer resistance. By drawing "homonormative" collective activity into conversation with more subversive retroactivism, I put pressure on the terms of queer rhetoric and the presentist impulse of some queer critics within and outside rhetorical studies to define what counts as queer resistance ex situ, in absolute terms. Instead, as I have argued elsewhere, we can intervene in this propensity "by examining the contingent, historically specific relations among locally enforced norms, rhetors, acts, and multiple audiences" (Bessette, "Queer Rhetoric in Situ" 148). A rhetorical understanding of "queerness" reads an act in a specific historical and rhetorical context with a nuanced understanding of the multiplicity of audiences, asking "Queer to whom? When? Where, and how? Normative to whom? When? Where and how?" (Bessette, "Queer Rhetoric in Situ" 157). As Cathy Cohen astutely reminds, differentials of power exist within all collectives, even those read as normative by contemporary queer standards. The DOB are both queer and normative, depending on who is looking, how, and when.

That differentials of power exist within and divide identity-based coalitions makes it all the more imperative to examine the rhetorical, retroactivist *work* that goes into shoring up and sustaining identity categories. Yet, as many scholars have pointed out, queer theory has historically been decidedly anti-identitarian. Duggan's coining of "homonormativity" represents a concern in queer studies that celebratory and normalizing lesbian and gay identity projects might blunt queer theory's ever-resistant edge. Nonetheless, this book advocates a return to identitarian projects. As Heather Love contends, such critiques of identity scholarship may have "short-circuited important critical work in the history of identity" (45).

Yes, Love explains, gender and sexual identity has proven to be deeply problematic, but it "nonetheless remains a powerful organizing concept in contemporary experience" (45). Rather than dismissing outright the concept of identity in our historical treatment of sexuality, Love argues that "we need an account of identity that allows us to think through its contradictions and to trace its effects. Such a history can offer a critique of identity without dispensing with it as a category of historical experience" (45). I endeavor to treat identity with the complexity Love advocates by attending to its "contradictions" and "effects," while honoring it as a tenacious concept in both history and individual subjectivity.

What Love's queer historiographic approach contributes to the theoretical underpinnings of this project is the insight that rhetorical constructions and contests over gender and sexual identity are not merely a *result* of retroactivism—they are also a "cause," as it were. Love asserts that "identity not only accounts for the shape of the past but also for the feelings [that queer subjects] continue to have about the past" (45). The composition of the past not only shapes identification—identification also shapes the composition of the past, through recognition; queer historiographers "are condemned to search for roots and resemblances" in the archives and historical record (45). In each study, recognition returns as a motivation for historiography. While Love, like Bravmann, is speaking to and about professional historians of sexuality and queer literary studies—that is, *academics'* recognition of themselves in the subjects they study—recognition of figures and experiences from the past is, as Burke suggests, a fundamental rhetorical function of identification.

Recognition is more complex than seeing oneself in the mirror of a historical figure or text, however. As Rohy explains, the "process of discursive identity-formation" is not merely an instance of the researcher finding herself in its pages or archives. It is really a "moment of invention, which retroactively creates the subject as *having always been* inverted, gay, deviant, queer, Uranian, trans, lesbian, or homosexual" (Rohy 355, her emphasis). Historiographic recognition is a process of instantiating oneself into a tradition that substantiates an enduring sexual subject.

This process is not necessarily conscious or intellectual. Indeed, Love suggests that recognition is unavoidable because it is emotional: "it is in large part because [queer subjects] recognize figures, emotions, and images from the past as like ourselves that we feel their effects so powerfully" (45). That is, despite intellectual and theoretical challenges to identity as a concept in queer theory, the emotional pull of recognition continues to hold sway. This affective dimension of recognition makes emotion an integral part of queer rhetorical, historical practice. As Cvetkovich argues, "lesbian and gay history demands a radical archive of emotion in order to document intimacy, sexuality, love, and activism—all areas of experience that are difficult to chronicle through the materials of a traditional archive" ("In the Archives" 110). Cvetkovich explains that emotions and sexuality can be archived only indirectly, through the mediation of cultural artifacts. The drive to recognition propels the rhetors' identification with a past into forms less traditional than official records or history textbooks.

As Cvetkovich suggests, queer challenges to evidence and archives disrupt conventional ways of thinking about the material form and media of history. José Esteban Muñoz advocates a concept of the evidence of queer history as "ephemera": a "modality of anti-rigor and anti-evidence that, far from filtering materiality out of cultural studies, reformulates and expands our understandings of materiality" ("Ephemera" 10). Ephemera and the "radical archive of emotions" (Cvetkovich, "In the Archives" 110) that serve as evidence in queer rhetorical practices make it impossible to limit what counts as history to traditional print volumes organized in narratives and punctuated by major events. History will be found and made with "whatever heuristic is at hand," as Elizabeth Freeman asserts ("Introduction" 62), necessitating an imaginative attention to the *media* of historical production that makes queer historiography possible.

For the collectives featured in this book, the past cannot be composed in the traditional narrative forms of linear cause and effect that occupied so much of Hayden White's influential philosophy of history, for lesbian pasts have always been elusive and elided in official archives and professional histories. Instead, the pasts these collectives composed take on diverse and unexpected forms and media, harnessing discursive, material, multimodal, and digital rhetorical strategies. Each chapter focuses on a different medium of historical production, ranging from printed newsletters, books, and correspondence to material archival collections to film and digital video. This approach to the media of historical production is premised on the notion that technology cannot be separated from our larger concerns in rhetorical studies, corralled in specifically technology-focused areas of study. Rather, as Stuart Selber maintains, "technological contexts have moved toward the center of disciplinary conversations and encouraged people to think expansively and sometimes untraditionally about their practices and perspectives" ("Introduction" 2). No longer the sole purview of the thriving areas of study that take technology as their explicit focus (namely, computers and composition and technical communication), these "technological contexts" have inspired new throngs of scholars to reconsider their methodologies, objects and scope of analysis, and even the traditional canons of rhetoric (see for example Enoch and Bessette; Brooke).

Advancing this disciplinary momentum, I attend to the technologies of rhetorical practice that the collectives in this study leverage, examining how lesbian collectives' rhetorical activities "technologize the queer archive," because, as Alexander and Rhodes maintain, a "variety of media are needed to (re)construct queer experiences." The technological differences between print, material archivization, film, and digital video and archives matter because each affords rhetors different strategies for composing and reaching their audiences. Technology is "directional," Carolyn Miller argues: "it appeals to us, by making some forms of communicative interaction possible or easy or others difficult or impossible, by leading us to engage in or to attempt certain kinds of rhetorical actions rather than others" ("Foreword" x). Like rhetoric then, or more precisely *with* rhetoric, technologies help shape the way pasts are composed and delivered. For example, while material archives encourage the selection and arrangement of an eclectic mix of artifacts and identifications, the technology of archiving does not encourage the *manipulation* of these materials. Instead, it encourages the *preservation* of individual materials, and the rhetorical work happens in the selection and juxtaposition of existing artifacts, with some care taken to preserve their individual provenance. In contrast, technologies of film and video encourage the *remediation* (Bolter and Grusin), manipulation, and even invention of archival materials.

These strategies depend on the availability of technologies of production for grassroots activists and independent filmmakers. As Susan Wells argues, the democratization of publishing technologies such as offset printing in the 1960s—to this I would add, handheld video cameras in the 1970s and personal computers and editing software in the 1990s—afforded new publication practices and opportunities for marginalized groups, such as collaboration, quick and easy document reproduction, and access by amateurs. While the emergence of these accessible technologies did not determine retroactivist strategies and style, lesbian collectives have fashioned technological features into affordances, shaping their rhetorical strategies through the constraints and possibilities of the technologies at hand. The democratization of publication technologies influenced the kinds of retroactivist invention and delivery the retroactivists employed, even as the rhetors exploited the technologies inventively for their purposes. Each technology of historical production afforded its rhetors different ways to mediate the past and impact their constituency.

And so this book proceeds across time and technologies of historical production. Despite the diversity of sources, the studies that constitute this book together demonstrate how these different groups, media, and strategies coalesce in the project of retroactivism. By bringing the more conservative aims of the midcentury DOB into conversation with the increasingly radical retroactivism of experimental documentary filmmakers, I set out to demonstrate that there is a legacy of retroactivism that has produced unique forms of sexually identified communities, inventive rhetorical strategies, and creative uses of technology in the production of lesbian historiography and identity. I hope that this project issues a challenge to feminist and queer historiographers to attend to how historiographic rhetoric functions in contests over identities and the historical forces that shape them.

1. THE DAUGHTERS OF BILITIS ARCHIVE

CLEARING HISTORICAL SPACE FOR CLUSTERED ANECDOTES

> We do feel that the experience of Lesbians, expressed in their own terms and in the context of their own self-awareness, has merit in and of itself. . . . This isn't just "our" book. It is the story of the many Lesbians we have met over the years.
>
> —Del Martin and Phyllis Lyon, *Lesbian/Woman*

> Your book is anecdotal, so it leads me in that vein too.
>
> —K. Elizabeth Jackson, letter to Martin and Lyon

Fifteen years after Del Martin and Phyllis Lyon founded the Daughters of Bilitis (DOB), they composed *Lesbian/Woman* (1972). This influential 283-page book is a collection of lesbian experience from hundreds of women the couple had corresponded with through their work with the DOB during the 1950s and 1960s. Though the publication punctuated the dissolution of the organization, the book continued the DOB's agenda to educate women with same-sex desire about themselves, to promote self-acceptance, and to encourage broader social acceptance through conforming to conventional middle-class values. By strategically collecting and curating the experiences of the many women with whom they communicated throughout the history of the DOB, Martin and Lyon hoped to extend the organization's particular sense of collectivity to women with same-sex desire across the country. Through this curatorial work, *Lesbian/Woman* came to constitute an *archive* of lesbian experience that functioned rhetorically as a communal and identificatory resource for readers. The book provided women without access to lesbian community or what it "meant" to be a lesbian a curated collection of experiences with which they could identify.

Viewing *Lesbian/Woman* as an archive with specific design and impact is premised on the notion that archives have "situated and strategic uses," as Biesecker has argued ("Of Historicity, Rhetoric" 130). Scholarly attention to their rhetorical implications has come to light over the previous decade, prompting Morris to express surprise in 2006 that "the archive itself, chief among inventional sites of rhetorical pasts, has not been subjected to sustained critical-rhetorical reflection" ("Archival Turn" 113). Since his remarks, the field has continued to devote attention to the archival methodologies of rhetorical historians (Glenn and Enoch; Ramsey et al.; Kirsch and Rohan); yet, fewer scholars have granted the "critical-rhetorical reflection" Morris urged to archives themselves, their design, and their impact.

To attend critically to the *Lesbian/Woman* archive as an "inventional site of rhetorical pasts" (Morris), I embark in this chapter on four intimately related investigations, beginning with the DOB's history of literate activity in their monthly magazine, the *Ladder*, and its influences on Martin and Lyon's later rhetorical design of *Lesbian/Woman*. Then I draw on queer theories of disidentification to argue that *Lesbian/Woman* cleared historical space for the experiences in the archive by diffusing the ambiguous sense of misrecognition in existing histories of homosexuality. Third, I investigate how the archive of *Lesbian/Woman* clusters DOB members' experience into a unique historical record. Extending scholarship on the ephemeral nature of queer archival materials, I consider the rhetorical construction of *Lesbian/Woman* as an archive of anecdotes: numerous, brief articulations of experience retold second-hand and curated in strategic categories. As in a more traditional archive with shelves, boxes, and folders, the anecdotes in *Lesbian/Woman* are set side by side with only the rare transition provided by Martin and Lyon. But *Lesbian/Woman* is not a typical archive, either in its contents—clustered anecdotes—or its form—a published book. Anecdotes, as Randolph Starn explains, have their "uses precisely in disrupting the detached pose and forced coherence of history-as-usual" (140). Consequently, collections of anecdotes such as *Lesbian/Woman* can amplify the single anecdote's unruly potential to disrupt cohesive accounts of lesbian stigma.

In tandem with this exposition of the rhetorical construction of the *Lesbian/Woman* archive, my fourth investigation examines how readers responded to and made use of its collections of anecdotes. The book inspired invention in its readers, who wrote dozens of autobiographical letters and sent them to Martin and Lyon from around the country.[1] The second epigraph to this chapter suggests the significance of the anecdotal archive for its readers. As K. Elizabeth explains in her letter to Martin and Lyon, "your book is anecdotal so it leads me in that vein too," before articulating her experience coming out in her "fire and brimstone background" and her struggle to accept her sexuality. The many letters like K. Elizabeth's evince the heuristic potential of archives to prompt a process of *archival consciousness raising*. Drawing on Tasha Dubriwny's theory of consciousness-raising and repurposing it in application to queer archives, I argue that the anecdotes in *Lesbian/Woman* validated readers' experiences and encouraged them to contribute to the archive begun by Martin and Lyon, effecting transformations of self-acceptance and attempts to forge community despite the frequently rural locales of the readers. However, these transformative effects were only possible for women who saw themselves reflected in the archive's anecdotes of middle-class women. I thus close this section with a reader's letter exposing the limits of *Lesbian/Woman*'s ability to inspire consciousness-raising for more diverse lesbian readers.

THE DOB IN CONTEXT: FROM MOBILIZATION TO ARCHIVIZATION

To understand the rhetorical design and impact of *Lesbian/Woman* as a queer archive, it is important to comprehend the political and cultural context in which the DOB mobilized. In 1955 eight women—four working-class, four middle-class—came together to begin a secret social club as an alternative to the San Francisco bar scene, desiring the privacy to openly dance with other lesbians without police interference. While gay and lesbian bars were the primary means of meeting and socializing with other women, public meeting places carried considerable risk in the era of McCarthy.[2] The bar scene was fraught with the peril of police harassment and arrest, the effects of which extended beyond punitive damage to the potential for a lesbian's sexuality to be exposed to her family or place of employment, often resulting in alienation or job loss. As Nan Alamilla Boyd explains, bars were targeted because they were sites where cruising, gender transgression, sex tourism, and prostitution coalesced; bars were, in other words, sites where lesbian difference was *visible*—visibly gender subversive and working-class—and where queer people fought to protect their right to visible difference in public spaces.[3] In contrast, the social club sought more private, less perilous opportunities for community.

Within a year of the social club's founding, it divided over its purpose and across class and race lines.[4] While most members opted to retain the club's social purpose, Martin and Lyon also wanted to combat what they understood to be a pervasive problem for lesbians: the pathologization and criminalization of same-sex desire, the resultant sense of isolation, and the lack of representation for lesbians in the burgeoning homophile movement.[5] Martin and Lyon, both white (and white-collar), left the social club to found the first activist organization for lesbians. Retaining the original club's name of the Daughters of Bilitis, the organization grew slowly as leaders mitigated potential members' fears of exposure. Through coffee meetings, conventions, epistolary correspondence, and their magazine, the *Ladder*, however, the DOB eventually expanded as chapters opened in cities around the country. A staff of volunteer DOB members edited and wrote the magazine, hand-typing and, often, secretly mimeographing and mailing copies from their places of employment.

Tracing the terminology in the *Ladder* shows a transition from self-identifying as "variants" to naming themselves "Lesbians," always with a capital L to indicate their identity as a collective, a people. This tracing indicates a gradual coherence of a particular identity, one that the DOB chose for themselves against the dispersing discourses of pathology and criminality.[6] The DOB's mobilization in the 1950s homophile movement marks a historical moment before lesbian identity had become visible and exclusively named, except by deprecatory medical discourse. At the time of the DOB's origin, women with same-sex desire were still pejoratively dubbed "variants" or "inverts" in psychological discourses, which contributed to a pervasive sense of isolation and individual pathology and consequently obstructed their collectivization into shared identification. As David Halperin explains, "Lesbian" did not become a "dominant or exclusive" name for a "particular kind of erotic practice or sexual orientation" until the latter part of the twentieth century (53).[7]

From 1956 to 1970, the DOB corresponded and conversed with women across the country to "communicate that same-sex attraction meant something, that it had social ramifications, and that it had a name" (Meeker 2), and it proffered the organization's primary message of self-acceptance as a foundation for lesbian community. The DOB's emphasis on self-acceptance led to later accusations of assimilationism and passive activism compared with more radical, post-1969 gay liberation protests. But in response to these accusations, Martin replied that "people need to have a sense of self-worth to fight for. What we were trying to do at that time is survive . . . to build a sense of community among those of us who could, that gave us self-esteem and . . . a sense of our own individual power—and then our power as a group" (qtd. in Boyd 153). Once a sense of community was forged against the isolating forces of McCarthyism, the final objective of the DOB was to encourage the mainstream to understand that, as Lyon explained, "there is really nothing to fear from us (for that is the true reason behind the prejudice—fear)" (qtd. in Meeker 83). To achieve this aim, the DOB called for collective conformance to mainstream expectations for feminine dress and middle-class sensibilities of respectable daytime occupations, moderation or abstinence from alcohol, and romantic monogamy, in the hopes that doing so might grant them relief from social and official harassment. For the DOB, these middle-class sensibilities were a strategic intervention in the common association of lesbians with pathology, crime, immorality, and mental aberrance and were expressly set against the gender and class transgressions of the bar scene.

In line with the earlier homophile movement, Martin and Lyon's archival prescriptions for social conformance were premised on appeals for privacy, promising compliance to middle-class values in exchange for relief from harassment. In contradistinction, the emerging gay liberation movement was moving away from requests for privacy toward demands to "publicize 'private' matters considered offensive to a phantom 'general public'" (Duggan, "Twilight" 53), manifesting the goal of publicity through demonstrations and mass resistance to bar raids. Also under way were increasingly factious strands of liberal, radical, and lesbian feminist activism.[8] By 1970 the DOB organization slowly dissolved as members became increasingly involved in these more radical feminist and gay liberation efforts.[9]

The DOB, however, did not end in silence. That same year, Martin and Lyon began to compose *Lesbian/Woman*, archiving the experiences of women they had known through the organization. To compose the book, the authors drew from the experiences women had written about and sent to the *Ladder* and from their memories of conversations and correspondence with hundreds of women through the DOB. Continuing the DOB's agenda, the *Lesbian/Woman* archive contains virtually no mention of bar experience, collecting instead anecdotes that shape a distinctly middle-class lesbian identity, characterized by values of monogamy, hard (respectable) work, femininity, and motherhood. Archives are not all-encompassing catchalls; they are constituted by decisions about what to include and how inclusions are arranged and categorized. The experiences collected in *Lesbian/Woman* are organized under categories—chapters—defined by these values. Within the ten chapters that make up the book, there are a chapter on motherhood ("Lesbians Are Mothers Too"), a chapter on monogamy ("Lifestyles"), a chapter on positive self-regard ("Self Image"), and a chapter on upbringing ("Growing Up Gay"). While the last two chapters focus on politics (the role of lesbians in the homophile movement and the burgeoning liberation movement), the majority of the book clusters snippets of the experiences of women who exemplified the middle-class values the DOB upheld.

ARCHIVAL LESSONS: LEARNING FROM ANN ALDRICH AND THE *LADDER*

Martin and Lyon were motivated to archive experience in *Lesbian/Woman* because they sensed a pervasive historical void for lesbians who identified against the queer bar scene and its class and gender diversity. At the time of their writing, the representations of lesbians available—primarily in sexological studies, sensationalizing pulp fiction, Sapphic history, and the historical nonfiction of Ann Aldrich—emphasized the *queerness* of lesbianism: the antinormative difference the DOB tried so hard to normalize.

Prior to Martin and Lyon's publication of *Lesbian/Woman* in 1972, Aldrich released the widely read nonfiction books, *We Walk Alone* (1955) (Figure 1.1) and *We, Too, Must Love* (1958), which interwove the stories of a few "cliques" of lesbians in New York City.[10] Unlike *Lesbian/Woman*'s anecdotes of monogamy, motherhood, and other conservative values, Aldrich's books detailed jealous, capricious women and loveless relations born in bars. Aldrich even elaborated the story of a cruel woman who "preyed" upon a scared, underage girl, "luring" her away from her friends at the bar to her apartment and then abandoning her after returning to the bar and finding that the girl's friends left without her.[11]

Aldrich's publications became a topic of heated debate in the DOB, who held meetings and devoted sections of the *Ladder* magazine to analyzing and discussing her work. The magazine's ultimate conclusion was that Aldrich "failed to balance her more bizarre examples of Lesbianism

Fig. 1.1. Cover of *We Walk Alone*, by Ann Aldrich (1955)

with those who have attained adjustment and are useful, productive citizens" (1957, 1.9, 16): a "failure" that revealed the need for a book like *Lesbian/Woman.* Helen Sanders, a DOB leader, wrote that she felt "Ann Aldrich quoted heavily from medical and psychological authorities who are very biased" instead of including the experiences of "real" lesbians (1957, 1.9, 17). By critiquing Aldrich, the DOB began to circumscribe their *alternative* understanding of history and identity. In an open letter to Aldrich published in the *Ladder,* Martin concludes that Aldrich had let the "extreme" examples represent the majority of lesbians, whom Martin argued were likely "capable of carrying on an intelligent conversation" without "bravado" (1958, 2.7, 4). In tracing the DOB's debate with Aldrich, a collective identity begins to emerge: the middle-class lesbian, characterized by romantic monogamy, education, socially acceptable employment, and modesty.

The debate with Aldrich also encouraged readers to publically share the intimate experience that would come to characterize the strategy of anecdotal clustering in *Lesbian/Woman.* The *Ladder* was mailed (discreetly in a plain paper cover) to subscribers all over the country and occasionally internationally, with each issue encouraging readers to write in to the editorial board with their experiences and perspectives. In response to Aldrich, readers wrote to the *Ladder* to share anecdotes of personal experience that contradicted Aldrich's representation of lesbians in the bar scene as pathologically noncommittal. M.L. from Warwick, Rhode Island, for example, wrote that she was "hurt" to find no lesbian couple in Aldrich's writing with which she and her partner could compare themselves: "my friend and I have lived together for less than five years but as far as we are concerned, it's for life. We own our furniture and car jointly and just signed a mortgage for a home of our own. . . . I wish Aldrich would write about someone like us" (1958, 2.8, 22). Like this reader, F.L. from Peacedale, Rhode Island, wrote that readers need to be provided with complex accounts that include both sadness and hopefulness, because facing "this life *without* the benefit of viewing what goodness there is is as unrealistic as she who knows only the beautiful" (1958, 2.11, her emphasis). The *Ladder* compiled these counterfactual experiences to reinforce the DOB's differentiation from Aldrich's world.

Readers' letters like these begin to suggest the influence of the *Ladder* may have had on Martin and Lyon's strategy of clustering anecdotes. Like *Lesbian/Woman*, the grassroots periodical incorporated and published the thoughts and experiences of its readers. As the second issue pleaded:

> A few people cannot educate the public and themselves but many can. Give us those thoughts which have been lolling in your brain. Your name needn't be signed in your letter, nor printed. Your innermost desire is to be 'recognized.' Well, you won't do it by thinking but by doing" (1956, 1.2, 7).

This call to readers speaks directly to the drive to recognition, the collective understanding that these women's "innermost desire" was to see themselves represented and affirmed as lesbians. Later issues continued to beg for reader-generated content: "We need . . . contributions. We need manuscripts, both fiction and non-fiction, by and about women to correct erroneous conceptions—to depict Lesbianism as it is, not as it is supposed" (Dec. 1956, 1.3). Readers complied, submitting their responses to previous issues in letters to the editor, as well as their interpretations of organization discussions and events, and their fiction and poetry. By compiling the contributions of DOB members in the magazine, the *Ladder* thusly functioned as a record of the experiences and opinions of DOB members who wrote to share their acclaim or disdain for articles and issues, and contributed their views on what lesbians were and how they should best navigate the social world. Martin and Lyon would later draw from this record of experience, as well as their memories of correspondence and conversation with women in their time as leaders of the DOB.

The "lesson" of clustering experience that Martin and Lyon learned from the *Ladder* is particularly apparent in the checks and balances readers provided the newsletter as the DOB grew and changed through the 1960s. While earlier issues included at least two pages of many readers' comments, later issues would skip the "Readers' Response" section altogether or would print one, longer letter, reducing the sense of collectivity effected by clustering many women's voices in an issue. The DOB's increased political activism through the late 1960s (as opposed to their longtime program of self-acceptance and education) filled the pages with descriptions of legal battles and injustices, leaving less room for readers' letters. When readers' letters were printed, they strongly resisted this change. J.C. from New York commented on the paranoia-inducing repetition of "grossly exaggerated Injustices and Slights on the part of the Hostile Public" and begged for more reader interaction. She wrote that she preferred the entire newsletter be filled with readers' voices, because it would be "more constructive and helpful if we could get *each other's* slant on things" (1966, 11.3, 27). Readers resisted what they saw as an editorial/DOB leadership takeover of what was once a collective project. Even members of the *Ladder* staff agreed: Gene Damon[12] wrote to the editor that "we need to hear less and less about meetings and more and more about people. What they do and say and feel and fear and love and want" (1967, 11.5).

Readers' resistance to the *Ladder*'s increasingly monovocal approach provided Martin and Lyon with an important rhetorical lesson: readers wanted to see themselves and each other, clustered together to evince the sense of community they deeply desired. DOB members wanted to feel like they were part of a collective, to have channels through which to converse with other lesbians because it was so difficult to find them, especially for women in small towns and women who avoided bars. As

Meredith Grey, a frequent contributor of short stories, wrote in a letter to the editor, "it is immodest and unwise to suggest that the DOB can, now or ever, dispense with dialogue" (1967, 11.4, 2).

This reflection on the role of Aldrich and the *Ladder* in the exigency and design of *Lesbian/Woman* suggests that *reading and writing experience* served a vital function in the DOB's collectivization of lesbian identity, which was composed against existing accounts. Women sought out and joined the DOB because they wanted information about themselves and each other as lesbians and, together, they revealed the damage inflicted by available research like Aldrich's books on these individuals' understanding of themselves.

DIFFUSING DISIDENTIFICATION

One simple lesson from Aldrich and the *Ladder* was that members of the DOB were readers, and they were invested in finding accounts of lesbians in which they could see, inform, and celebrate their sense of themselves and their desire. Rohy suggests that this "intense library cathexis" should not cause surprise: "Those whose difference is antifamilial, somatically unmarked, culturally veiled, and potentially shaming are drawn to lonely stacks and secret research, where the archive enables self-definition" (355). Before clustering anecdotes in strategic normative categories, *Lesbian/Woman*'s first two chapters acknowledge this drive to research, as Martin and Lyon recount their own experience seeking to understand emerging feelings of same-sex desire by visiting gay bars ("always a twitchy experience," they claimed) and spending hours in the library, where they found little except a "few books about the male homosexual" (11, 29).

Instead of love, Martin read that her feelings for Lyon were a "perversion, a sign of psychopathology, a crime against nature and a sin against God" (30). Existing accounts had an emotional impact:

> All this is what Del learned about herself after hours of agonized reading at the library. They were talking about her, a Lesbian. And they were right. Lesbians do suffer from feelings of rejection, loneliness, isolation, fear, insecurity, hurt pride, lack of self confidence, loss of self esteem. Del felt all these things and more. She was indeed sick. She displayed all the symptoms of melancholia . . . [but] how could it be otherwise? The realization that she is considered sinful,

> criminal, and mentally ill can be overwhelming and devastating to a young mother of twenty-five [years], particularly when she sees what she experiences as simply a state of being and expression of love (49).

As Martin and Lyon suggest in this passage, the library sources were *persuasive*, convincing Martin that perhaps her feelings of love might not be love at all but deviance. Martin's reflection on the affect of available research illustrates her sense that the sources might *cause* melancholy, rather than merely empirically observe it in women with same-sex desire.

Martin's ambivalent identification with sources in the library partially resembles the queer rhetorical practice of disidentification: "the ways in which one situates oneself both within and against the various discourses through which we are called to identify" (Alexander and Rhodes). Disidentification is a feeling of misrecognition, an "uneasy sense of standing under a sign to which one does and does not belong," as Judith Butler first explained in *Bodies That Matter* (219). Thus the "dis" in "disidentification" and the "mis" in "misrecognition" do not mean that queer readers feel wholly foreign and distinct from the historical figure or description; "dis" and "mis" in this context mean that the identification and recognition are muddled, scrambled, both identified and not.

This complex sense of disidentification as a misrecognition is important in understanding the persuasive impact of available research on women with same-sex desire in the 1950s and 1960s, and the rhetorical context in which *Lesbian/Woman*'s archive set out to intervene. As Martin's experience illustrates, women seeking information about themselves *saw* themselves in the library, even as they felt they didn't or shouldn't, because there was no other archive from which to learn and it was difficult to locate other women with same-sex desire, especially for those who lived in small towns or rural areas.

For Muñoz, there is some potential for resistance in the experience of disidentification. He explains that the "process of disidentification scrambles and reconstructs the encoded message of a cultural text in a fashion that both exposes the encoded message's universalizing and exclusionary machinations *and* recircuits its workings to account for, include, and empower minority identities and identifications" (Muñoz, *Disidentifications* 31, my emphasis). For example, a queer black woman might identify with some of the politics of radical feminism or anticolonialism even as she doesn't when those politics ignore or deny nonnormative sexuality, and she can harness this disidentification for a queerer intersectional politics (*Disidentifications* 9). But the DOB, invested as they were in shaping a lesbian identity against associations with deviance and the queer bar scene, sought instead to *diffuse* disidentification, to clear space for an archive with which their presumed middle-class readers might more fully identify.

Instead of harnessing the queer rhetorical practice of disidentification then—that second step of Muñoz's where the queer rhetor "recircuits" the message to "empower" herself—Martin and Lyon set out to neutralize the persuasive impact of available sources. The authors used the first chapter of *Lesbian/Woman* to clarify disidentification with available research: to reduce its power as an identificatory resource for DOB members and to make room for their own archive of anecdotes. They did so primarily by excavating conflicting accounts of lesbian deviance, setting them against each other, and asking readers to consider how anyone could stand beneath such an incoherent sign; perhaps, Martin and Lyon imply, it is not the readers who are "scrambled" but the sign itself.

Lay researchers driven to learn more about their desire often came across accounts of Sappho, the poet from Greek antiquity who lived on the isle of Lesbos. As Martin and Lyon explain, Sappho has been reconstructed in historical accounts in multiple, contradictory ways. While she was celebrated in some accounts as a founder of a school for young girls, in others she was remembered as the predatory leader of an island cult for female homosexuals. The ambivalence of disidentification was built into the contradictory accounts of Sappho's history; one Sappho was "the great poetess and the other the courtesan of undisciplined habits" (Martin and Lyon 20). To clear historical space and relieve the affective impact of disidentification, Martin and Lyon emphasized and exploited the conflicting accounts, arguing that their contradictions called into question the historical accuracy of either version. If there could be "two Sapphos," then neither constructed account was likely to be equal to Sappho herself. Further, the authors demonstrated that Sappho's multiple configurations in history had present consequences, as her contradictory accounts led to negative associations with lesbians ranging from childish romantic to prostitute to child molester (21). The message in the opening chapters is clear: Martin and Lyon understood available accounts of lesbian history to be *rhetorical, contradictory, motivated, and malignant*, impacting women with same-sex desire who saw themselves in Sappho's many images even when they believed they should not. Indeed, the collective's naming after

Sappho's (fictional) contemporary, Bilitis, despite Sappho's ambiguity in the historical record, suggests the pervasiveness of disidentification for the group.

The authors used the same deconstructive strategy to discredit sexological studies found in the library by women with same-sex desire.[13] These studies were printed in nationally distributed publications purporting to illuminate the public about lesbians with claims about their physical and mental deviance. For example, Dr. Hugh Barnes's article "What Makes a Homosexual?" was published in the 1957 issue of *Actual Medical Cases*, arguing that lesbians have "firm muscles" and "excess hair," with "over-developed" stature and "underdeveloped" femininity—a hypermasculinity at odds with the DOB's encouragement of normative femininity. To diffuse disidentification with sexology, Martin and Lyon once again exploited the contradictions between accounts by juxtaposing Barnes's claims of physical deviance with the opposite claims of a Dr. Edward Dengrove. In a contemporaneous issue of the journal *Sexuality*, Dengrove characterized lesbians as "essentially feminine" with no marked difference in appearance. But where he denied physical difference, he proposed *psychological* deviance: "for most Lesbians are not women who are pretending to be men, but rather women who cannot express their normal sexual drive in relationship to men but must direct it towards other females instead" (qtd. in *Lesbian/Woman* 19). For Dengrove, lesbians had abnormal sex drives and gender confusion but were physically and essentially "women." In short, where Barnes saw physical deviance, Dengrove did not, and where Dengrove saw psychological deviance, Barnes did not. Martin and Lyon simply used each study to discredit the other, and to support their contention that, like Sappho's histories, medical perspectives on female homosexuality were fractured and contradictory.

Even while the sexology studies were published in accessible popular journals, their claims found greater circulation in pulp fiction, the inexpensive paperbacks sold in newsstands. The pulps were a lucrative business for writers, including Aldrich, who is credited with writing the first mass-marketed pulp about lesbians under the pseudonym Vin Packer in 1952.[14] Like some accounts of Sappho, including the tale of her student, Bilitis, many midcentury pulps perpetuated notions of lesbians as sexual predators of the young and innocent. In sensationalized paperback accounts, girls were often initiated into sex by older, more experienced women. The pulps followed other common plots as well: prostitutes who found diversion with other women; rich housewives who mitigated boredom with their maids; imprisoned women who found solace in their cellmates from their isolation from men. The pulps were a major source of disidentification for women with same-sex desire in midcentury—Nestle, the founder of the Lesbian Herstory Archives, even calls these texts "survival literature" because they were embraced as a life source as the most accessible representations of lesbians available at the time; they were proof that lesbians existed, even if the sensationalized tales perpetuated associations of lesbians as predatory and oversexed.

For Martin and Lyon, the pulps were evidence of the malignance of classical historical and sexological accounts, because stories manifested Sapphic myths and sexological claims of lesbian gender transgression. Martin in particular was not immune to the disidentification provoked by available fiction. Writing about Radclyffe Hall's novel *The Well of Loneliness*, the authors describe how "many women, like Del, emulated" female protagonist Stephen Gordon's performance of masculinity—her brusqueness, her fierce need to protect women. Del did, and did not, see herself in Gordon's performance of gender, but more importantly her partner *Phyllis* did not (or did not want to) see Del in Gordon: the women who mirrored Gordon would only find that "their lovers, like Phyllis, were not looking for a male substitute, for lesbians are attracted to women" (*Lesbian/Woman* 12). Even if readers saw themselves in Stephen Gordon without disidentification, without the simultaneous sense they did not, Martin and Lyon assured them that real lesbians *should* not, for as their title asserts, Lesbians are also /Woman. This particular act of diffusing disidentification and clearing historical space is a clear attempt to define a more normative (read: feminine) gender identity.

These early pages of *Lesbian/Woman* clear space of the contradictory clutter of Sappho, sexology, and sensational fiction, making room for a new archive—an archive of DOB women's own experiences with femininity, hard work, romance, isolation, and unrequited love. Instead of historical accounts that claimed lesbian pathology, DOB women's experiences of *reading and learning* about lesbian pathology become part of the content of the queer archive that is *Lesbian/Woman*. In other words, the historical material the book contained was no longer pieced together from sexology and Sappho; instead the affective experience of that failed research became part of the content of a new lesbian history, encapsulated in *anecdotes* from DOB members and curated in strategic categories. The next brief section develops a rhetorical theory of "anecdotal clustering" as a consciousness-raising historiographic strategy before delving into the anecdotes themselves.

RAISING CONSCIOUSNESS FROM A QUEER ARCHIVE OF ANECDOTES

Martin and Lyon made it possible to fill their archive with anecdotes by diffusing disidentification with Sappho, sexology, and the pulps and undermining them as reliable and authentic representations of lesbian history. As Freeman maintains, instead of deferring to experts, professional historians, and sensational fiction, queer people have had to make sense of their lives through less conventional means: through "gossip," "conjecture," and "ephemera" (62). Echoing Freeman, Muñoz writes,

> Queerness is rarely complemented by evidence, or at least by traditional understandings of the term. The key to queering evidence, and by that I mean the ways in which we prove queerness and read queerness, is by suturing it to the concept of ephemera. Think of ephemera as the trace, the remains, the things that are left hanging in the air like a rumor. (*Cruising Utopia* 65)

Indeed, queer pasts are by nature difficult to preserve because they are often legible only as desire, as love and intimacy, as performance, as activism. Because official archives, libraries, and histories have corrupted, forgotten, or elided queer pasts, queer archives must be composed with contents and in forms that do not look like the official paper records we expect archives to contain.

In approaching *Lesbian/Woman* as an archive of lesbian experience, I extend the concept of queer archival ephemera to consider *anecdotes* as a form of historical evidence. Anecdotes are ephemeral because they are experiences articulated secondhand and retold in absentia of the subject whose experience is divulged, with no material record to authenticate it. Each anecdote in *Lesbian/Woman* is a moment in another woman's life without bildungsroman, plucked from a past organized by linear time, origin, and telos and inserted into categories elsewhere. Martin and Lyon assure readers that the experiences they relay come from the "thousands of women" they "talked to, counseled, socialized with, and been friends with" during their decades of DOB leadership (*Lesbian/Woman* 9).[15] But the anecdotes in *Lesbian/Woman* are experiences temporally delayed and retroactively transformed: the experiences were endured and felt by DOB members and the *Ladder* readers at the time they were shared with Martin, Lyon and other DOB constituents in the 1950s and 1960s; later, in 1970 as Martin and Lyon composed the archive that would become *Lesbian/ Woman*, they collected these experiences and reorganized them secondhand. Because of the distance between the retelling and the experience, anecdotal ephemera is "a kind of evidence of what has transpired but certainly not the thing itself" (Muñoz, "Ephemera" 10).

An anecdote is a brief form, and particularly so in *Lesbian/Woman* where anecdotes are often comprised of a short paragraph or a few sentences. They are typically light on details: in the book, for instance, the anecdotes refer to the women Martin and Lyon describe only by their first names, revealed as pseudonyms to protect the women's privacy. In contrast to similar forms like the "example," the anecdote does not evidentially support an assertion in *Lesbian/Woman.* Instead, the anecdote itself shows, rather than supporting a statement that tells; each anecdote exists for its own sake, next to others' anecdotes, rather than in service of an explicit claim. Here is an example of an anecdote in the chapter focusing on motherhood:

> One couple, who had a definite butch-femme relationship in their youth, had wanted a child so badly that they made various attempts at artificial insemination without success. Many years later, when they were in their forties, they eagerly greeted us with the news that they had had a baby. They had adopted the baby of an unwed mother in Lillian's family. By that time, Bo, the butch, was less obvious as a Lesbian and more obvious as a successful businesswoman. The couple had a spacious home with a swimming pool outside the city. (*Lesbian/Woman* 156)

This anecdote reinforces several mainstream values for Martin and Lyon: it celebrates the couple's wish for motherhood; it suggests a long-term, monogamous relationship between women; it favors the "butch" partner's conformance to more feminine gender performance; and it implies that happiness is found in economic success and suburban life. Yet there is no definitive interpretation of the anecdote provided by Martin and Lyon. Instead, "Lillian and Bo's" anecdote is preceded by "Delia's" and followed by "Judy's" related experiences becoming mothers in the face of legal and cultural obstacles. Together, these anecdotes suggest a conformance to conservative values.

This normative conformance was strategic, as the anecdotes were meant to intervene in the existing accounts of lesbian deviance. In historiography, anecdotes have the effect of disrupting a single grand narrative. As Lionel Gossman colorfully declares, "like an ideal human form when it is inspected close up through a microscope, the heroic and orderly public narrative of the history is undercut by a ragbag of anecdotes of depravity" (152). Because of their unruly potential, anecdotes are distrusted in "mainstream history," claims Starn, who says the "default position is that anecdotes are a guilty indulgence unless severely disciplined"; the "jarring anecdote" effectively upsets the "detached pose and forced coherence of history-as-usual" (140). The collection of experiences in *Lesbian/Woman* from so many unofficial or hearsay perspectives had the potential to disrupt the dominant narrative of lesbian pathology, criminality, and moral deviance.

It is in this sense that the *Lesbian/Woman* archive of anecdotes is distinctly rhetorical: the strategic collection and curatorship of lesbian experience had specific, *interventionist* effects on its readers' understanding of themselves as lesbians by undermining the pejorative official narratives in which they had sought information about themselves and providing a collection of experience in their place. The evidence of the anecdotal archive's effects can be found in the dozens of letters sent to Martin and Lyon in response to *Lesbian/Woman*. Many of the women who sent letters to Martin and Lyon lived in rural towns and small cities in the American midwest and south, far from the hubs of liberation activism then flourishing in San Francisco, Los Angeles, and New York City.[16] These readers found little in the way of research or lesbian bars, but the archive of anecdotes offered them an alternative account of lesbian experience in which they could see themselves or to which they could aspire.

The *Lesbian/Woman* archive inspired a process of archival consciousness-raising in these readers. "Consciousnesses" are "raised" when the composition of a multiplicity of experiences connects what was previously felt individually into the foundations for collective identification and action. The famous feminist dictum, "the personal is political," means that personal experience, when shared and linked with others' experiences, reveals that individual suffering is a product of systemic problems. As Karlyn Kohrs Campbell explains, the goal of consciousness-raising is "to create awareness (through shared experience) that what were thought to be personal deficiencies and individual problems are common and shared, a result of [women's and, here, lesbians'] position" ("Rhetoric of Women's Liberation" 128). *Lesbian/Woman*'s archive of anecdotes did "not simply alter opinions" but created a "situation in which the telling of individual experiences makes possible a reframing of one's understanding of the world" (Dubriwny 396)—a reframing of individually felt guilt, fear, and visible difference into self-acceptance and adherence to middle-class conventions of dress, behavior, education, and occupation. Because this reframing encouraged conformance to social mores rather than critique, it does diverge from feminist liberation consciousness-raising in this sense. But, by comparing their experiences to the linkages of DOB women's experience in the archive, readers came to view their personal trauma not as a result of individual pathology but rather the result of a world hostile to same-sex relations. They then leveraged their resulting self-acceptance to seek community with other like-minded lesbians.

As Dubriwny explains, consciousness-raising requires both the "validation of experience by others" and the "necessity of the telling of their own experiences by individuals" (401). The *Lesbian/Woman* archive drew together the experiences of many women to collectivize a lesbian identity in which these isolated readers could see themselves, validating their experiences and compelling them to contribute accounts of those experiences to Martin and Lyon's archival categories. As one reader, Pamela, from Albion, Washington, explained in a letter to Martin and Lyon, "I'm reading your book for the second time and, *as a result, I have to write*" (emphasis mine). The archive encouraged the sharing of private disclosures across the miles and the years, which many readers saw as less dangerous than sharing with unsympathetic friends and family. This remote sharing was especially true for readers in small towns or cities without flourishing feminist and gay liberation activism, lesbian bars, or the ability or desire to locate them—readers who frequently lament in their letters that they have "no one else to talk to" and no other way to find information about themselves as lesbians. Martin and Lyon collected experience from a host of women with same-sex desire until a collective identity was palpable enough to dispel the common sense of isolation and individual pathology, thereby inviting readers to contribute their own anecdotes to the archive.

FORGING COMMUNITY FROM ANECDOTES OF FAILED RESEARCH AND UNREQUITED LOVE

When juxtaposed with readers' autobiographical responses, *Lesbian/Woman*'s collections of anecdotes illustrate the archive's heuristic potential to inspire invention and transformation in its readers. Though *Lesbian/Woman* contains a breadth of categories and hundreds of anecdotes, most readers responded directly in their letters to two particular collections of anecdotes on which I focus here: the failure to find information about lesbians in conventional places and experiences of unrequited love and romantic monogamy.

Failed Research as an Inventional and Communal Resource

In *Lesbian/Woman*, the experience of searching for information and failing to find it actually became a *resource* for identification with other lesbians, supporting Cvetkovich's contention that "trauma can be a foundation for creating counterpublic spheres rather than evacuating them" (*Archive of Feelings* 15). Through compilations of anecdotes, Martin and Lyon attempted to transform the negative affect of failed research by suggesting that the experience can actually build community. The authors curated the anecdotes of "Joyce and Marty" who "walked into the DOB national office looking for information about Lesbianism" after being expelled from the military for rumored lesbianism (202). The women sought out the DOB because they did not know what lesbianism was, could not find information in conventional places, and wanted to know if they were indeed what the military accused. The brief anecdote about Joyce and Marty is then followed by an equally brief anecdote of another woman's experience: "Maggie's," who was grateful to the Navy for edifying her about her sexuality. The short paragraph devoted to Maggie describes her appearance—she was a "tall, lanky, and masculine appearing woman"—and uses reconstructed dialogue to re-create the experience. Previously unaware of her sexual preferences, Maggie was questioned by Navy officials and called a "butch." She remembered to Martin and Lyon, "'I couldn't figure out what he was talking about, and he didn't believe me, so he wouldn't tell me.' She grinned. 'After I got out, I found out though'" (202). The brief account of Maggie's military experience constitutes an anecdote because it represents an encapsulated moment, incorporates reconstructed dialogue to emphasize the oral transmission of such "historical" evidence, and exists in a moment in time, later recollected and shared with Martin and Lyon, who still later relay the experience secondhand.

The anecdotes make collective what might have been an individual trauma. An anecdote like Maggie's expresses one women's simple, humorous memory of her failure to find information about lesbianism, but because her story is archived with Joyce and Marty's, who also needed the DOB to explain what lesbianism was to better understand their expulsion, Maggie's experience is collectivized, shown to be experienced by *women* accused and expelled from employment without explanation. Maggie's anecdote contradicted dominant accounts that would call her maladapted (she "grins," after all, in memory of military pressure), and her anecdote, with Joyce and Marty's, illustrated to readers that the military's strict prohibition of homosexuality—and their refusal to share information about the meaning of their accusations—could backfire by informing women with same-sex desire that there were others like them to whom categories such as "butch" applied.

Maggie's anecdote is immediately followed, with minimal transition, by "Tillie's," "Georgie's," and "Jackie's" similar but slightly different experiences of sexual self-understanding and the discovery of lesbian community as a result of the military's denigration and expulsion. For example, Georgie and Tillie were discharged from the military for "association," even though they did not actually have a relationship. After Tillie was discharged, her family sent her away out of shame. The twenty-year-old went to the city where Georgie lived and they turned to each other for support and love (203). Martin and Lyon imply that rather than merely exposing it, the military's expulsion actually *drove* her to a same-sex relationship.

Like Starn and Gossman's characterization of anecdotes as unruly and subversive bits of history, these anecdotes functioned in the *Lesbian/Woman* archive as a counter to perceptions of lesbians as necessarily melancholic and isolated. The women's anecdotes showed them to collectivize in response to accusations—to seek information from others who may be like them (the DOB) and, in so doing, to learn that their desire had a name and potentially an identity. Because Martin and Lyon rarely intervened with transitions or explanations between the anecdotes, lesbian readers addressed by the book were prompted more through induction than deduction, assembling the mass of anecdotes as they read. Often without direct instruction on how to make use of these anecdotes, readers drew their own connections between anecdotes and perhaps mentally added their own to the category.

Several dozen readers wrote letters echoing the failure to find information and adding their anecdotes to the category containing the experiences of Del, Joyce, Marty, Maggie, Tillie, and Georgie. One woman wrote,

> Just as you all . . . searched the literature for information, I too searched articles and books on psychology, fiction, etc. for more knowledge about myself. What I read I partly accepted as gospel because of the aura surrounding psychology, but I knew most of us didn't fit its descriptions and analyses.

Carol from Plentywood, Montana, wrote requesting "any material, books, [and] newsletters" because "there isn't too much material on lesbians in this town!" Still another writer, Mary from Cleveland, Tennessee, wrote that she, "like Del, trundled off to the library. Would you believe that in my county of 51,000 persons, we have one small library . . . and that in that library there is *one* reference to lesbianism and it consists of one chapter in a heavy tome on Freud." As the military women did in their archived anecdotes, the letter writers came to Martin and Lyon to share their confusion about lesbianism and to seek information.

Because Martin and Lyon clustered anecdotes of similar experiences of failed research, each one functioned as a "kernel story" begun by Martin and Lyon, effecting the connections between experiences necessary for consciousness-raising. Each anecdote "supports" the other experiences in the archival category, helping to "achieve the tone of harmony in the group"; in response, readers added their anecdotes to "fit the topic under discussion" (Kalcik 8). By archiving multiple women's experiences of failed research, including Martin's own, *Lesbian/Woman* inspired readers to contribute their own experience to the category, "reshaping the meaning of that individual experience" (Dubriwny 398) from a lonely ignorance to a *shared* indignation.

Isolation, Rejection, and Unrequited Love as a Collective Problem

This shared indignation at the dearth of information about lesbianism provided *Lesbian/Woman* with an ethos for the other categories of experience archived in the book. Positioned as a response to silences and biases in traditional archives and libraries, the experiences collected in the book were meant to fill the void of information and community in the library and for women without access or interest in lesbian bars. The categories under which Martin and Lyon assembled anecdotes reflect the archive's function as counterevidence to pathological accounts in psychological texts. For instance, in the chapter titled "Lifestyles," Martin and Lyon assembled anecdotes of more than ninety women who "live quietly unassuming lives and expect fidelity from their partners" (112). This chapter collected the experiences of lesbians that contradicted psychiatric accounts of excessive sexuality. Introducing the collection of anecdotes, Martin and Lyon described the irony, and isolating force, of this accusation:

> This stereotype [of excessive sexuality] often turns a quiet life into one of quiet desperation and brings about a turning away from sex and/or involvement with other Lesbians simply because such noninvolvement seems the only "safe" way to survive in a hostile society. It is ironic (but consistent with America's confused view of sex) that a large number of people whom society would castigate for sexual variation, i.e. Lesbians, actually don't engage in sex at all, or do so very rarely. We have known a number of women who fit this category: women who have identified themselves as Lesbian, who suffer through all the fears that they may be found out, that they may lose their job, that they may face rejection from friends and family, and yet have never found either the woman or the nerve to change their status from one of being to one of doing. (94)

Citing the experiences of the many women they have "known," Martin and Lyon simultaneously refuted accusations of excessive sexuality as a product of "America's confused view of sex" and circumscribed lesbianism within mainstream expectations for feminine chastity and modesty. They attributed the pervasive sense of isolation and individual pathology felt by women with same-sex desire to the dispersing effects of accusations of promiscuity.

To combat this dispersion, Martin and Lyon archived the anecdotes of a dozen middle-class women who dreamed of monogamous love with another woman but instead isolated themselves out of fear. "Ann" was a schoolteacher who lived a "self sufficient but lonely life, untouched by human hands" because she "built a shield around herself" (95). "Elsie," a highly ranked social worker, feared losing her job and maintained a "nonsexual involvement with a circle of friends," while "Charlotte" could never share her feelings with her unrequited love, "Gert," out of fear of rejection. In Dubriwny's terms, each experience was "unique," but the "similarities in their stories became visible because each story emerged" after earlier anecdotes (406). The similar but subtly divergent anecdotes of "Beulah," "Zelda," "Marnay," "Wanda," "Sally," "Merle," "Jean," and many others underscore Martin and Lyon's intention with the archival category: to express that "by and large, most Lesbians opt for one-to-one, long-term relationships as an ideal" (97). Even when Martin and Lyon included an anecdote suggesting promiscuity, they condemned it in their retelling of the experience. "Kate," for instance, was "much too bold and flirts with danger constantly," almost losing her office job after being reported to her supervisor for making passes at her colleagues (96). For Martin and Lyon, Kate was another example of a "loner," denied lasting love because of fear.

In return, letter writers almost universally responded to the middle-class values of long-term romance and fidelity, adding to the archive of experience their own anecdotes of self-isolation, fear of rejection, and dreams of love. Bonnie from Columbia, Missouri, for instance, described her satisfaction with her "good job as a producer-director of instructional media, television, and film" but feared she would never meet a life partner. She offered an anecdote of her recent rejection by a woman who had "developed a very cold hard view of human relationships. She had been rejected by someone else she had loved and had been in other bizarre relationships." Bonnie shared her own fears of becoming like her lost love, turned to "stone for the sake of self-preservation." She compared *Lesbian/Woman* with *Sappho Was a Right-On Woman* (Abbott and Love), which was published in the same year of 1972, finding Martin and Lyon's book superior because it didn't "try to tell me *how* to be gay" by requiring her to flout monogamy. She did not want "anyone telling me a monogamous relationship is inherently bad anymore than I want anyone to tell me I'm sick because I'm a Lesbian." Bonnie found Martin and Lyon's book "less judgmental and dogmatic" because first, her own aspirations for lasting love were already mirrored in experiences of the women in its archive and, second, because the clustering of anecdotes did not tell her how to be a lesbian as much as it shared the experiences of a number of lesbian women in whom she could see herself.

Like Bonnie, Deborah from St. Catherine, Ontario, described how her relationship was troubled by fear and isolation. She fell in love with her roommate, Wanda, but the "guilt and fear of discovery instilled by society" overtook her. She did not "fit in" with the gay men and lesbians she met in a rare bar experience and was not sure she had the "strength of character necessary to live my life as these people [in the bar] seemed to be doing." As a result of feelings of guilt and fear, her relationship with Wanda began to strain and they "stopped going out socially for fear that people might think we were 'those type' of women," likely referring to bar-going women of lower class and masculine dress. Nearly every letter Martin and Lyon received shared an experience with unrequited love or rejection and the desire for long-term monogamy.

The isolating effects of these painful experiences frequently resulted in intense depression and self-loathing. After a breakup, Kathy from Duquesne, Pennsylvania, tried to deny "the existence of my lesbianism and also the existence of myself," resulting in "bouts with bottles and with pills" to put herself in "another world." Each woman, like Sherron from Ashland, Kentucky, described "frustration and confusion," "self-hatred and despair." Sometimes, these painful experiences led to alcohol and drugs. Carol from Plentywood, Montana, thought they would

> meet my every need of feeling good about myself but then [drugs and alcohol] too destroyed the very little self-worth I managed to have left after living a life continually surrounded by the armed guards of guilt, shame, fear, resentment, isolation and loneliness. Not only did I think of myself as a piece of trash, a social outcast, because I was a lesbian, but I was also drinking way too much and doing any kind of drug I could get my hands on.

These women were compelled to share intimate anecdotes of pain with Martin and Lyon, because the letter writers could already see themselves in Martin and Lyon's archive. Mary from Cleveland, Tennessee, had struggled with accepting her sexuality for eight years until, "there in the pages of your book, in black and white, I saw myself." Mary's experiences of unrequited love and longing were "validated," in Dubriwny's terms, as *lesbian* experience by *Lesbian/Woman* and by her own articulation in response. The painful individual experiences took on new meaning as a collective problem faced by lesbians as a result of dispersing discourses of guilt, fear, and isolation; rather than an individual pathology, readers began to see their now collective isolation as a result of erroneous but pervasive social perceptions of lesbianism.

Forging Self-Acceptance and Middle-Class Collectivity across Racial, National, and Regional Lines

Lesbian/Woman did not only archive experiences of pain, isolation, and fear in the aspirations for monogamous love. Following the assemblage of anecdotes that suggest a collectivity of isolated women, Martin and Lyon countered with even more anecdotes of women who had managed to find lasting love and only wish to sanctify it with marriage, providing evidence that relationships were possible for lesbians who accepted themselves and reached out to others like them. "Joyce" and "Madeline" were joined in a "celebration of commitment" at an Episcopal church. Martin and Lyon recalled that "Joyce was jubilant when she broke the news to us. This tall, pensive, sensitive young brunette had been through years of struggle with her parents, her church, and her psychiatrist. Finally she had received the blessings of all three to be herself" (99). Martin and Lyon's retelling of Joyce and Madeline's story is replete with the language of experience: it represents the emotions of Joyce and Madeline (their eyes "brimming with joyful tears") and the solemn sanctity of their voices ("I give you this ring as a token of our covenant, vowing to live in close friendship . . . to love you even as I love myself. May God be between me and thee forever.") Though Joyce emerges as a unique individual, she is also representative of conventional marriage more generally, with vows that pledge love, faithfulness, and support under God. This identification with mainstream, middle-class, heterosexual women—who were not accused of excessive sexuality—was meant to emphasize the injustice committed against lesbian women and to diminish negative associations with promiscuity, prostitution, alcoholism, and other social transgressions attached to female homosexuality. Joyce and Madeline's anecdote is followed by a string of other couples—"Neva" and "Judith," "Marjorie" and "Tracy"—who had found enduring love, failing only to celebrate it with state-sanctioned marriage.

The archived experiences suggest that middle-class values reigned supreme as the cohering factor, allowing for the inclusion of women of color and international women's experience as long as their anecdotes reflected the DOB's core values, like monogamous love. Interspersed among the many anecdotes of apparently white, monogamous lesbian couples, Martin and Lyon curated the anecdote of "Manonia" and "Donna," a black lesbian couple whose love and courage drove them to attempt to obtain a marriage license, and an anecdote of "Monty" and "Darlene," a black couple who struggled to stay together after Monty was "forced . . . by her married brothers and sisters" to move home and care for her ill mother because her own relationship was not as valid to her siblings as their own (101–5). While the DOB sometimes dissuaded gender transgressive or bar-going lesbians from joining the organization in an effort to shape feminine identification—which historian Martin Meeker notes is "almost surely evidence of brewing class antagonism in the lesbian world"—women of color were more readily accepted as long as they adhered to the collective aspiration for middle-class status and gender conventions (101). Indeed, one black lesbian held leadership positions in the DOB—Cleo Glenn Bonner was a circulation manager for the *Ladder* and was elected national president in 1964 (Meeker 102). But the acceptance of black lesbians as members and leaders and the inclusion of their anecdotes in the *Lesbian/Woman* archive did not entail, as Meeker asserts, an "active explor[ation] of the intersections of race and sexuality" nor a "clear understanding of how lesbianism might be experienced differently by women of color even if class status was shared" (102).[17]

The inclusion of anecdotes from international women also focused more on similarity than difference, emphasizing the shared desire for monogamous love. But, more than with respect to race, anecdotes of international women's experience did acknowledge the unique conditions for female homosexuality in different national contexts. "Ger," for example, a lesbian from Indonesia, "wanted love" with another woman but felt "coerced" into heterosexual marriage due to customarily strict expectations and the comparatively more pointed humiliation and banishment resulting from transgression. She married a man for three short months before "revolting against captivity and breaking free" (*Lesbian/Woman* 128). Ger, as in so many anecdotes of American women in the archive, remembered feeling isolated, as if she were the only woman with feelings for other women. But ultimately, Martin and Lyon concluded that, "though customs and language may differ from country to country, Lesbians are pretty much the same around the world"; Ger wanted love and found it in "Hetty," a woman with "sharp features and cat-green eyes" (129). Ger's anecdote reinforced the archive's implication that lesbians across the world share the same desires for commitment and suffer similar stigma, secrecy, and isolation despite differences in race or nationality, contributing to the sense that lesbian experience is *collective* across (some) differences.

The juxtaposition of failures to achieve monogamous love with examples of the many women of various races and nationalities who had overcome these failures had an apparent transformative effect for the reader-writers. The letters frequently followed a rough pattern, beginning with the articulation of experiences of isolation, depression, and unrequited, lost, or struggling love that the letter writers saw mirrored in the archive, and closing with claims to "self-acceptance" based on the evidence provided in the archive of middle-class women who managed to find and keep life partners. As Dubriwny explains, "collective rhetoric takes place through the validation of experiences," and, here, the validation of the experiences to which these relatively diverse women aspired—lasting love. This validation is "one way oppressed groups rename—and hence create new meaning from—their experiences" (Dubriwny 396). The letter writers' experiences of loss and their dreams of love were validated in the archive's anecdotes, helping them to rename their experiences from an individual pathology to a collective struggle and to generate new meaning—"self acceptance"—from them.

The generation of self-acceptance from this renaming allowed even the drug- and alcohol-addicted letter writers (whose addictions might have excluded them from the mainstream aspirations) to see themselves in the archive. Carol from Plentywood, for instance, wrote that she was recovering from her addictions and that "just admitting and accepting my disease of alcoholism and chemical dependency gave me the same sense of relief and freedom that I felt when I admitted to myself and others that I was a lesbian." She proclaimed that she was a "grateful alcoholic, drug addict, woman, and lesbian" and that "through these painful experiences, I have found and continue to find the greatest blessing . . . me . . . Carol, a human being." Kathy from Duquesne, Pennsylvania, admitted that she had known for many years what her "sexual preferences" were but could "never fully accept them even though I have had several lesbian relationships"; after reading *Lesbian/Woman*, she realized she was living in denial: "I don't know what title I had for loving women . . . but I can now say "lesbian" and like the word, how it sounds and what it means."

These letter writers effected this transformation in the composition of experience, and then leveraged their transformed sense of self-acceptance and lesbian identity to forge new contacts with other lesbians. In each case, after sharing their experiences of depression and isolation and their transformation to self-acceptance, the letter writers made moves toward creating community, toward replicating in person the sense of collectivity they saw in the archive. The archive of anecdotes in *Lesbian/Woman* inspired the letter writers to share their experiences with Martin and Lyon and, when possible, more local community. Bonnie, for example, believed that it was "reading . . . about all the woman who have contacted" Martin and Lyon that encouraged her to "try as well to somehow reach across the void to my sisters. I want to know if I am unique in discovering the growing fear of women in relationships to get involved and risk part of themselves." The letters suggest that the archive helped create community by demonstrating the affirmation of lesbian experience between participants, a community readers now wanted to extend to physically and temporally local lesbians. Readers closed their letters with promises to change introverted behavior and often sought help from Martin and Lyon in locating lesbians "like them" in their region, that is, lesbians with little interest in or access to the bar scene. Eileen from Ashland, Kentucky, wanted "desperately to get in touch with some organization near enough for me to talk to people, to meet people. I don't think I'm the kind of person who'd feel comfortable going to bars." Marcy pleaded for "any contacts you can give me. I'm living in a small town in Minnesota and, believe me, there isn't much to do. There is a small gay bar in Sioux Falls, South Dakota, but the chance of meeting other women is small." Several letter writers expressed a willingness to travel more than one hundred miles to meet other lesbians if Martin and Lyon could only provide them with references.

THE LIMITS OF THE *LESBIAN/WOMAN* ARCHIVE

The anecdotal archive of *Lesbian/Woman* resonated with middle-class women letter writers, who frequently mentioned in passing undergraduate and graduate degrees, and careers such as nursing, teaching, television production, and higher education. Their articulated experiences reveal women who disidentified with the visible gender, sexual, and class transgressions of the bar scene and felt the consequent isolation of their *invisible* same-sex desire. While this audience is clearly self-selecting—seeking out *Lesbian/Woman* and voluntarily composing letters—it is also clear that the authors crafted their archive to reach this contingent of women with same-sex desire, invoking their audience through the curating of anecdotes and categories. Though anecdotes, as I have argued, have the potential to disrupt dominant historical narratives, the archivization of *Lesbian/Woman* suggests that collections of the form might also create a new grand narrative, one that challenges heteronormative narratives but, in doing so, instantiates a homonormative history in its place. Just as Martin and Lyon illustrate the damage caused by heteronormative historical narratives of pathology and stigma, one reader's letter suggests the damage caused by the archive's social conformance. This reader's difference stands out and exposes the limits of *Lesbian/Woman*'s ability to inspire archival consciousness-raising in a more diverse group of lesbian readers.

Virginia, a prison counselor from Jonesboro, Arkansas, initially praised the book as the "most honest book on gay women" she had read but immediately transitioned into the intense confusion the archive of lesbian experience had caused, not calmed, in her. Unlike the experiences of isolation and unrequited or lost love felt by the other letter writers, Virginia's lesbian experience was from the beginning social and, in her mind, socialized: "since I came out in the bars [in the bigger city where she went to university], my gay orientation is in that realm of flaunting homosexuality with the devil may care attitude [*sic*]." She was a self-described "butch—in the fullest sense of the word" and recounted in her letter her experience transitioning into masculine dress and manner in emulation of the "only models" she "had in the bars." Virginia shared in detail the permanence of this socialization: her self-identification as a man, her discomfort in women's clothes and mannerisms, her hatred of her female body. Her experience, in other words, did not add to the archive Martin and Lyon had composed but directly challenged it; she was aware that her anecdotes would have no place among those she read. As she astutely explained to Martin and Lyon, "you said in your book that the real purpose of the DOB is to help lesbians adjust to life as *women*—well, I do not even think of myself as a woman anymore." But rather than dismissing the archive as containing the experiences of lesbians who identify differently than her, Virginia struggled to find ways to fit in its categories.

Virginia wanted to see herself in *Lesbian/Woman*'s archive because she did identify with some of its middle-class aspirations for employment and romance. She believed that if she wanted to "live in this straight society and have a good life" and "to work at the profession I was trained for . . . without the hell I'd have to face if the world knew I was a lesbian," then "I have to *act* the part of a single, feminine woman." Her "wife," Terry, also objected to her butch dress and behavior because Virginia internalized the roles and projected them on their marriage: "I've always played the role of the man and the husband . . . to the full degree and I've expected her to fulfill my needs as a wife to the full degree." Terry, like the women in the archive, did not have preconceptions about gendered roles in lesbian marriage, but Virginia laments several times that she knows no other way to relate to her partner:

> I just don't understand how two lesbians can live together in a marriage without butch/femme roles. Isn't one of you more aggressive or dominant than the other? Is this not butch? Doesn't one of you do things wives do and one of you do things husbands do? . . . I know my butch behavior is learned, but I don't know how to unlearn it and learn to think of myself as a woman.

Rather than decide that Terry and the archive were incompatible with her sense of self and relationships, Virginia became apparently depressed and confused by the incongruity between what she was and what she wanted. She and Martin and Lyon exchanged a few more letters, but Virginia seemed little consoled in the end.

Ultimately, for Virginia and perhaps others like her, *Lesbian/Woman* did not effect the rhetorical process of consciousness-raising, because her experience was not validated by the archive. Her own experiences were in fact *in*validated by the archive even as it cohered with her aspirations for employment and monogamy, and so she could not transform the experiences into a collective struggle and, finally, self-acceptance. She was left even more isolated than when she began reading *Lesbian/Woman* because, like the women in the archive, she (no longer) related to "bar people" and felt they had "very little in common" with her, despite her previous patronage of bars. And, after reading the archive of experience in *Lesbian/Woman*, she now felt that her butch identity—previously a social orientation in bars—was the individual pathology, not her same-sex desire. The archive (and Terry) had succeeded in dissuading her from bars and gender transgression but had left her without the resources to embody femininity nor find new community.

Virginia's location in Arkansas might have limited the range of options she could imagine or realize and may have made it more difficult for her to resist her sense that the archive contained the experiences she should have and the woman she should be. Women in cities like San Francisco, where gender transgression and sex roles were more accepted, may have found it easier to find queer community. For example, in contrast to Virginia, San Francisco bar owner Rikki Streicher was able to maintain a stronger resistance to the DOB:

> I remember Phyllis and Del marching up . . . and Del said . . . "Why don't you join this organization, Rikki? You know there's no reason for you not to—" and I said, "because we have nothing in common." And she said, "What do you mean we have nothing in common?" I said, "I have nothing in common with those women. You know I'm over here [in the bars] . . . my whole attitude and approach to life is different from theirs. I'm not beating the same drum." (qtd. in Boyd 161)

Unlike Virginia, Streicher was securely situated in an urban community of visible class and gender difference; unlike Virginia, her employment—the success of her bar—depended on this community and her obvious membership in it.

Somewhat paradoxically, Streicher's anecdote reveals and reinforces the *rhetorical* construction of *Lesbian/Woman*'s archive of anecdotes. Despite Streicher's assessment of difference and distance from Martin, Lyon, and the DOB, the dialogue she recalls actually reveals a familiarity between her and Martin and Lyon that exposes their social interaction in reality. Indeed, in their own oral history interview with Boyd, Lyon admits that they frequented lesbian bars—far more than their published accounts like *Lesbian/Woman* would indicate. According to Boyd, the DOB "depended upon bar life—the central artery for queer life—for their activities" and met many of their friends there (160). Martin and Lyon's silence about this aspect of DOB life in the *Lesbian/Woman* archive was a strategic omission, an attempt to distance their identity textually from their actual participation in the bar scene. They wanted to be remembered as private, middle-class, socially acquiescent citizens, and they wanted this activism to continue to reach new lesbian audiences through the rhetorical effects of the published archive. Martin and Lyon's choice not to include anecdotes from bars in the archive was a rhetorical strategy against the public conceptions of lesbians that emerged in part from the bar culture's predilections to gender transgression, late hours, alcohol, and casual affairs. Inadvertently, however, this strategy worked against people like Virginia, who identified with some aspects of bar culture and some aspects of the DOB.

CONCLUSION

Martin and Lyon were so confident that their strategy of clustering anecdotes in *Lesbian/Woman* might have the collectivizing effects of consciousness-raising that they stalwartly defended their rhetorical choices to their first press, McCall's. Their editor, Susan Stanwood, criticized the authors' "superficial" approach to representing experience, calling the anecdotes "much-too-brief thumbnail examples of what happened to so-and-so." These "sketches," Stanwood contended, were "too slight to give the reader a sense of the individual under discussion," and so she recommended that the authors limit their examples to the lives of ten or so individuals with more detail about each instead of glossing several hundred individuals—a "dollop of Jane here and Susie there is meaningless," she quipped.

But Martin and Lyon refused to comply, seeking out another press in San Francisco's Glide Publications after their McCall's contract was terminated.[18] The authors may have refused McCall's demands because the task of expanding some anecdotes and omitting others would turn the anecdotes into case studies of individuals, ceasing to be anecdotes at all and reducing the number of "participants" in the collective rhetorical project of the archive. In contrast to Stanwood's prediction that brief anecdotes would lack meaning for readers, the letter writers suggest that it was as much the sheer volume of experience packed into the *Lesbian/Woman* archive as the content of the experiences that evinced the sense of community across time and place: filling the historical void, helping readers transform their feelings of guilt, fear, and isolation into self-acceptance, and encouraging them to find more local community with other lesbians. Indeed, transforming anecdotes into case studies, a genre with more detail and a more traditional form of proof, might have attenuated the queer archival investment in the ephemeral, and so Martin and Lyon sought another publisher.[19]

Despite the volume of experiences it contains, *Lesbian/Woman* still risked exclusion and confusion for gender transgressive or otherwise nonconformist women. Martin and Lyon's strategic categories provided little room for lesbians like Virginia, the prison counselor from Jonesboro, Arkansas, whose experiences were not validated but instead contradicted by those in the archive. In spite of or, more precisely, because of the conservative categories and experiences housed in *Lesbian/Woman*, the archive managed to reach a large number of women geographically distant from the lesbian, gay, and feminist activism flourishing at the time of its publication in 1972.

The different rhetorical effects of *Lesbian/Woman* for Virginia versus the other letter writers illustrate how even queer archives with expansive and ephemeral notions of evidence risk exclusivity because of the very rhetoricity of archives. All archives are rhetorical, I have maintained, because archivists must make decisions about what to include and how inclusions are classified. Queer archives too must make decisions about what counts as historical evidence and even who counts as lesbian: is same-sex desire enough? Or must sexual contact be proved? What constitutes such historical proof? Where does homonormativity belong in queer history?[20] Indeed, archives' reliance on classification to select and organize materials may challenge the very notion of queerness, which orients against the circumscription of individuals into categories, even consolidations of nonheterosexual identity. As Mathias Danbolt maintains, "a queer archive may . . . almost seem like a contradiction in terms, because if we understand identity to be essential for an archival order, the strength of queer theory is the continual pushing and troubling of such categories and definitions" (34). A queer archive is always at risk of collapsing under the force of one of its terms.

These cautions do not diminish the transformative effects for the readers of *Lesbian/Woman* showcased in this essay. These women's understanding of themselves and their community was deeply changed by the archive's curating of experiences. But the questions I pose do point to the ways queer archives in particular require more "sustained critical-rhetorical reflection," as Morris charges of archives more generally ("Archival Turn" 113). We must attend more closely to how the rhetoricity of archives constrains or constructs queerness as these archives endeavor to fill the historical void for queer subjects, because queer archives can provide significant inventional resources both for self-understanding and community building *and* identificatory confusion and solitude. In the next chapter, I take up this project in a study of the rhetorics of retroactivist, place-based archive collectives.

2. CLASSIFYING COLLECTIONS

SUBVERSIVE SCHEMAS AS *TOPOI* IN PLACE-BASED ARCHIVES

> Our concept of an archives must be different; we are different.
>
> —Joan Nestle, "Notes on Radical Archiving"

> [T]hink of the *topos* . . . as an aid to pattern recognition, specifically as a region that permits or invites the connection between the abstract and the concrete, between a pattern and the material in which it is instantiated, between *eidos* and *hyle.*
>
> —Carolyn R. Miller, "The Aristotelian Topos"

Twenty years after the origin of the Daughters of Bilitis in San Francisco, the Lesbian Herstory Archives (LHA) was born on the opposite coast. In establishing a place-based archive in New York City in 1974, LHA's founders set out to make history on their own terms: to assemble and preserve accounts of lesbian pasts that were being elided in public discourse, official histories, libraries, and archives. As cofounder Joan Nestle has proclaimed many times over, this archive did not preserve evidence of lives on the basis of their prominence or adherence to any prescription of gendered sexuality; instead, "all lesbians were worthy of inclusion in herstory" and "if you have the courage to touch another woman, you are a famous lesbian" to the archive ("Will" 1998, 228). With this expansive and inclusive philosophy of selection, LHA had, and retains, as its mission an explicitly retroactivist commitment to challenging and augmenting the available sources—the archives and libraries—from which damaging histories were written and lives erased.

In contrast to the Daughters of Bilitis, which was the only known American lesbian organization at its midcentury origin, LHA was not alone in its mission in the mid-1970s and early 1980s. Six years after

LHA's founding, the West Coast Lesbian Collections was established in Oakland, California, and soon moved to its current home in Los Angeles. There it was renamed the June L. Mazer Archives (JLMA) by coordinator Bunny MacCulloch in memory of her lover, June, who had recently passed away. JLMA has had a mission remarkably similar to that of LHA, seeking out and preserving the "cares, struggles, successes, and joys of everyday, just-trying-to-get-by Lesbians" (*Making Invisible* 9).

The similarities in mission between LHA and JLMA are no accident. As Lynn Fonfa, a founder of the West Coast Lesbian Collections, wrote in 1982,

> The inspiration to organize a lesbian archive came out of our work in the lesbian community and as collectors for and users of the Lesbian Herstory Archives in New York. The LHA instantiated the rediscovery of and commitment to lesbian history as a means of strength and a way of knowing the women who had come before us.

Following LHA's 1974 founding, many place-based archives were formed in the late 1970s and throughout the 1980s from Florida to Tennessee to Connecticut.[1] Though New York, the Bay Area, and Los Angeles were hubs of gay liberation and feminist organizing during this period, retroactivist archives dotted the United States, some of which remain open: in 1978 the still active Ohio Lesbian Archives was founded in Cincinnati by the staff of a local lesbian newsletter, and in 1974, the New Alexandria Lesbian Library was founded in Chicago—two months before LHA.[2] Amid the vigor of gay liberation and feminist activism in the 1970s then, *retro*activism flourished in place-based archives like these.

Focusing primarily on two of the largest and best-known American lesbian archives founded in this period, LHA and JLMA, this chapter investigates the rhetorics of retroactivism designed and leveraged by place-based archives. More than merely repositories of sources for other rhetorical histories, archives like these are themselves rich sites for rhetorical analysis (Glenn and Enoch; Morris, "Archival Turn"; Sharer, "Disintegrating Bodies"). For Biesecker ("Of Historicity, Rhetoric"), the rhetoricity of the archive came into view through feminist historiographers' rereading of the historiographic biases that had shaped the rhetorical tradition as a lineage of male theorists and rhetors: if historiography can be gendered and rhetorical, so too can the archives that select, arrange, and make available its sources. Following the deconstructive work of Jacques Derrida and

Dominick LaCapra, Biesecker concludes that archives "anchor nothing absolutely," that the past is not "in the archive, not in any archive, not even in all the archives added together" (127). And yet, while we may not find unmediated history in the archives, we will find rhetoric. The archive is a site that works to authorize itself as the objective foundation of history and, to do so, conceals its gendered, rhetorical construction. This concealment makes it especially exigent for rhetorical analysis, for as Biesecker asserts, "what the archive cannot authenticate absolutely but can (be made to authorize nonetheless)" is an "invitation to write rhetorical histories of archives" (130). Place-based archives are rhetorical constructs that are crafted through decisions about which materials to seek out and accept and how those materials are organized in the physical space.

These rhetorical decisions become a driving force in the archives' retroactivisms. Through decisions for selection, arrangement, and outreach, both the LHA and JLMA collectives sought to shape and preserve a multivalent, fluid lesbian identity that is radically inclusive and flexible. LHA is open to both lay and academic visitors from all over the world and "belongs," as Nestle asserts, to a vast and complex group of women with same-sex desire that exceeds any "one group of lesbians" ("Will" 1998, 233). The archive's collective of volunteer "archivettes" keeps their understanding of gender and sexuality dynamic and flexible by "actively sorting out documentation of the lives" of women as varied as "lesbian factory workers, butch-femme communities of the forties and fifties, lesbian prostitutes and sex performers" (Nestle, "Will" 1998, 233). Lest visitors think that LHA's sex positivity would exclude more conservative lesbians from its collection, they also house a large collection of materials from the Daughters of Bilitis, whose approach to retroactivism tended more toward conformance to the mainstream. The LHA collection reflects all of this diversity in the range and juxtaposition of its material objects: "hard hats and hobnail boots sit next to pasties and glossy prints of a famous lesbian stripper of the fifties. They, in turn, are joined by the lesbian-feminist artifacts of the 70s" (Nestle, "Will" 1998, 233). JLMA is likewise expansive in its holdings, ambitiously endeavoring to collect and keep "anything a lesbian has touched," resulting in collections full of letters, periodicals, photos, buttons, t-shirts—even a worn, holey pair of dirty sneakers formerly owned by MacCulloch.

And yet all of this diversity in identity and artifact is housed within explicitly separatist collections—these are not "gay *and* lesbian" archives.

Through the associations drawn between the distinct categories that organize the archives' holdings—all contained within the purview of "lesbian herstory"—visitors are encouraged to expand their understanding of and relationship to lesbian identity. If all of this eclectic diversity in LHA can be *lesbian*—even the controversial inclusion of some bisexual and trans materials in each archive, as I'll discuss later in this chapter—then the result is a dynamic queering, to "continually reconstruct the words 'woman,' 'lesbian,' and 'gender'" (Nestle, "Will" 1998, 233). Such radical inclusivity is a central tenet of these collectives' retroactivism, because the collectives are working against the bias and erasure of lesbians in official archives, libraries, and histories.

To make sense of the complex rhetorical activity involved in this retroactivist work, I argue that these queer rhetorical decisions are fundamentally classificatory in nature, for they depend on a schema that delineates which materials are appropriate for inclusion in the archive and into which folders, boxes, and shelves the materials are categorized. In this chapter, I theorize classification as a rhetorical *topos*, extending Miller's articulation of *topoi* as "conceptual shapes or realms" that serve to aid in unanticipated pattern recognition ("Aristotelian" 141). As I will demonstrate, the classification *topos* in these retroactivist archives blurs the boundaries between archival categories, creating the conditions for a generative, flexible identity.

To develop this argument, I begin by contextualizing the origins and exigencies for LHA and JLMA's retroactivism. I then theorize how classification functions as a *topos* in material archives and identify rhetorical strategies through which the archival classification system encourages a haptic research experience and the association between seemingly disparate and diverse materials in each archive. I close with an investigation of the limits of these archives' radically open definition of *Lesbian* by examining the positioning and inclusion of nonwhite, bisexual, and trans materials, the unacknowledged gaps in the archives, and JLMA's recent affiliation with a major academic institution.

CONTEXTUALIZING PLACE-BASED ARCHIVAL RETROACTIVISM

Before delving into how classification functions as a *topos* and the specific rhetorical strategies employed by these archives to encourage cross-categorical association, it is important to first explicate the context and exigency that motivated their mission and design: why did grassroots lesbian archives proliferate in the midseventies and early eighties and why were place-based archives in particular chosen as the medium of their retroactivism?

The Lesbian Herstory Archives was founded in 1974 by Nestle (a writer and lecturer at Queen's College) and her then-partner Deborah Edel (a psychologist), inspired by their participation in a lesbian-feminist consciousness-raising group at the 1973 Gay Academic Union conference. The Gay Academic Union was a liberation-era organization committed to making education more hospitable to lesbian and gay teachers and students, and for some academics it served as a gateway to joining liberation efforts. As gay historian John d'Emilio recalls, the Gay Academic Union is what led him to become involved in gay liberation activism writ larger, which in turn infused his academic work with more political consciousness (ix). At this conference attended by independent and university scholars, activists, and graduate students, LHA was born in the intersection of academics and liberation activism, which may have contributed to the retroactivist focus on *history*, on writing, and on archives. However, despite these origins, LHA has been from the beginning resolutely grassroots, community-based, and opposed to academic and institutional intervention.

While—as I will elaborate below—a primary exigency for these lesbian archives was in the erasure and bias in official libraries and archives, it bears mentioning here that another exigency—one that shaped the separatist ethos of LHA—was in the gender politics of the Gay Academic Union and the narratives of gay history that were already being shaped in the aftermath of the 1969 uprising at the Stonewall Inn, a gay bar in New York City. Within the Gay Academic Union, Nestle and Edel could already see factions within gay and lesbian activism, evident in the consciousness-raising groups that quickly divided into "sexist gay men, Marxists, and lesbian-separatists" (Nestle, "Will" 1998, 227). Nestle and Edel, who participated in the latter two groups, were particularly concerned that the vibrant pre-Stonewall lesbian culture from the 1940s and 1950s that had nourished them was disappearing from memory. The Stonewall Riots were quickly becoming positioned as the "absolute beginning, the zero degree" (Piontek 10) of gay culture and activism, with the consequence of eliding preexisting queer culture. The 1970s also witnessed a proliferation of lesbian and feminist publishing, and the consciousness-raising group knew that those grassroots "presses and publishers were fragile creations," with "precious productions" that needed active preservation (Nestle, "Will" 1998, 227). Seeing memory loss both within and outside gay and lesbian activism helped motivate LHA's separatist approach to retroactivism. In contrast to gay male- and lesbian-inclusive archives like the ONE National Archives, founded earlier in Los Angeles in 1971, LHA was decidedly of, for, and funded by the lesbian community.[3] As longtime volunteer Polly Thistlewaite explains, "LHA founders saw lesbians as a people and sought to congeal a lesbian identity and community, distinguishing lesbians both historically and culturally from straight women and gay men" ("Building" 153). By 1976 the archive (then housed in Nestle and Edel's upper-Manhattan apartment) was open to this community.

Like LHA, the June L. Mazer Archives has been committed to representing and serving lesbians. This archive was founded in Oakland, California, in 1981 as the West Coast Lesbian Collections by Cherie Cox, Lynn Fonfa, and Clare Potter, who were inspired by their volunteer work at LHA and wanted to create a similar resource center on the West Coast. After a few years, the then-defunct archive went into storage until June Mazer and her partner, Bunny MacCulloch, collaborated with local lesbian organizations[4] to move the collection into their Altadena home and then to the archive's current West Hollywood space.

Why did these community activists and educators choose *archives* in particular as the medium for their retroactivism? The answer reveals a primary exigency for both archives' founding and mission: the role of the archive in the history of politics, power, and nonnormative sexuality. As I have argued, archives are not merely places where documents naturally assemble due to their inherently preservable worth; they are shaped by rhetorical decisions of selection and arrangement. But more profoundly, archives are, as Michel Foucault contended, "the law of what can be said," the system that "governs the appearance of statements as unique events" ("Historical *a priori*" 28). Foucault is describing the power of the archive to produce what it is possible to know and say, and to authorize a happening as a bounded "event and thing" worthy of remembrance that could otherwise be forgotten. Events and individuals, in other words, can *achieve* status by virtue of their preservation in an official archive. As Achille Mbembe asserts, the archive is

> fundamentally a matter of discrimination and selection, which in the end results in the granting of a privileged status to certain written documents and the refusal of that same status to others, thereby judged "unarchivable." The archive is therefore not a piece of data but a status. (20)

The consequences of the difference between documents with archival "status" and those that are "unarchivable" are considerable. A foundation of authorization, the archive stands behind scholarly research, democracy and government, and, for Irving Velody, their claims to "ultimate truth, adequacy, and plausibility" (3). Jacques Derrida goes so far as to contend that "there is no political power without control of the archive" and that "effective democratization can always be measured by this essential criterion: participation in and access to the archive, its constitution, and its interpretation" (3). In line with these notions of archival power, LHA's first newsletter (1975) proclaimed that the purpose of the collective's existence was to "uncover and collect our herstory denied to us previously by patriarchal historians in the interests of the culture which they serve."

These grand claims about how archives can serve and reproduce normative interests manifest more concretely in the *classification* of queer materials in official libraries and their rhetorical impact on subjects driven to research their desires and identity. As Foucault explained, the "events and things" that gain status by virtue of the archive are not accumulated in an amorphous mass; rather they are "grouped together in distinct figures, composed together in accordance with multiple relations, maintained or blurred in accordance with specific regularities" ("Historical *a priori*" 29). For researchers from professional historians to queer individuals seeking evidence of their history, the archival process has wielded its power both through omission of documents that would make queer lives and activity enunciable in Foucault's sense *and* through systems of classification that organized materials around categories of pathology, crime, and immorality.[5]

Until the activist efforts of the American Library Association's Task Force on Gay Liberation in 1972 (figure 2.1), the Library of Congress and Dewey classification schemas closeted or pathologized queer materials by either omitting them from the collections entirely or classifying them within categories such as disease and sex crimes (Thistlewaite, "Lesbian and Gay Past"; Wolf; Adler; Carmichael). Texts tagged as "Homosexuality" were cross-referenced with crime, pornography, prostitution, sexual perversion, and psychological disorders. For example, libraries referred researchers of "homosexuality" or "lesbianism" to a general heading, "sexual perversion" (Thistlewaite, "Lesbian and Gay Past" 10). Librarian Steve Wolf demonstrated in 1972 that similar associations were made through cross-references in classifications of medicine: under "Sexual Deviation" was "Homosexuality," under which was the obligatory note, "Cf. HQ 71–79, Sex Crimes." Even after the Task Force's intervention, Wolf maintained that "Cf." referral notes remained in the Library of Congress system, which linked homosexuality to categories of crime and disease. For example, under "RA 1141: Sexual Offenses and Diseases," was the note "Cf. HQ 71–471, Sex Crimes." Since "Homosexuality" was classed in HQ 76, it fell within the range of the "Sex Crimes" classification numbers. The Cf. note implicitly grouped same-sex intimacy with crime *and* disease, alongside the "related" subjects of Prostitution (HQ 101–440) and Pornography (HQ 450–471) (figure 2.2). The Dewey decimal classification system contained biases comparable to those of the Library of Congress, using a "See . . ." cross-reference procedure: under "Homosexuality" were the entries "Crime, *see* Offenses; Sex, *see* Sexual Disorders" (Wolf 40–41).

For Wolf, a member of the Task Force on Gay Liberation, the system's biases exposed the Library of Congress as an "unthinking prop for an official Sexual Orthodoxy which does not depict the way things are, only the way the Orthodoxy would like them to be" (43). The "orthodoxy" of a classification system comes from whom it circumscribes as its assumed audience. According to feminist library science theorist Hope Olson, Charles Cutter's 1876 *Rules for a Dictionary Catalog* was a governing source in library categorization, and his influence lives on in his circumscription of a singular "class of people who use the library," a homogenous audience with shared perspectives and social standing. After Cutter, the Library of Congress continues to make decisions about language through their presumption of an imagined public's "habitual way of looking at things," even when they revise their subject headings over time to account for changes in this public (Cutter qtd. in Olson 55). The principle underpinning the system is what Rawson would call an "archival logic" of "efficient access," wherein the imagined public of researchers can most quickly and predictably locate what they are looking for ("Accessing Transgender" 136). Classification systems with this archival logic are meant to convenience

Fig. 2.1. Group portrait of Del Martin and Phyllis Lyon (*top row, second and third from right, respectively*), and members of the American Library Association's Task Force on Gay Liberation holding gay-themed books in 1972. *Photo by Kay Tobin; copyright © Manuscripts and Archives Division, The New York Public Library*

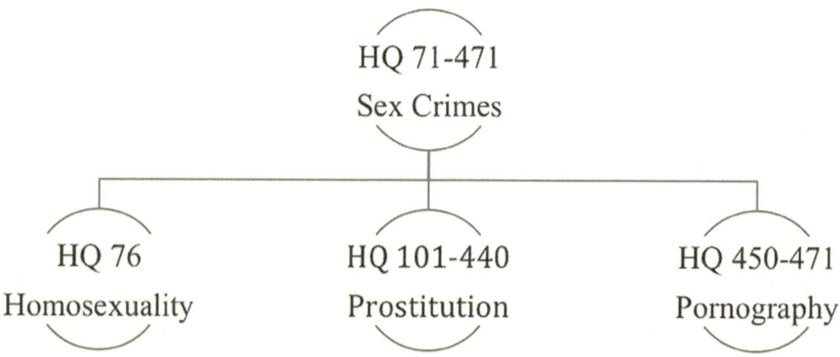

Fig. 2.2. Library of Congress classification, according to Steve Wolf (1972). *Diagram by author; source: Wolf, "Sex and the Single Cataloger"*

and anticipate the thinking of the normative public, but in doing so, this public's perspective can be imposed on those it excludes; as Olson puts it, the "authority of the 'public' is the authority of an established mainstream perspective, reinforcing the status quo" (56). This example of the Library of Congress as an authoritative, powerful archival system further evinces the rhetorical nature of classification because it makes clear that the system has an imagined audience and that classifying for this audience dictates organizing principles that reproduce the boundaries, and reinforce the assumptions of, that audience.

As Library of Congress subject headings have long been employed pervasively in libraries and national bibliographies worldwide (Olson 54), the normative identification of homosexuality with categories of crime and disease was not benign in the lives of queer people in the 1940s through the 1970s who often turned to libraries for information about their emerging sense of their sexuality. For researchers from professional historians to individuals with same-sex desire seeking information about themselves, traditional classification systems effectively rendered documentation of queer lives invisible or pathological with significant effects on subjects' sense of self and identity. JLMA's MacCulloch recalled in 1986 that there "wasn't anything" to read about homosexuality when she was coming of age—only the "abnormal psychology, Kraft-Ebbing, Ellis bunch of stuff"; like Daughters of Bilitis founder Martin and her damaging experience with research in the library, MacCulloch "did read all that then, but it was always about men and they might add a line or two—'well, perhaps there are women.'" (MacCulloch, interview). While MacCulloch claimed that she knew she wasn't perverse like the library materials suggested, Nestle's experience with available materials (and their absence) was more affecting:

> When I first loved women in the late 50s, I was living the life of a colonized subject. I did not know it then; I thought it was accidental that I found no references in the surrounding culture to lesbian creations. Sometimes believing the colonizers' view of myself, I did not even search for markings because I knew we were not a people, just deviant and sad wanderers, meeting in dark places. (*Lesbian Herstory Archives Newsletter*, 1975)

Later, in 1998, Nestle recalled "all the years the library had been part of the problem—its card catalog a journey in self-hatred for a curious 'homosexual'" ("Will," 1998, 235).

Martin's, MacCulloch's, and Nestle's isolating experiences in searching for "markings" in the library underscore the import of the archive in the formation of identification. Persuaded by absent or only pathological research, they identified not as "a people" (a collective identity) but as "deviant and sad wanderers"—dispersed and diseased. JLMA's current president, Ann Giagni, adds another dimension with her own experience researching in the libraries when she recalls surveillance and chained-up stacks: "While my generation was not as closeted as the generations before," she writes, "I am old enough to remember the police noting our license plate numbers when we entered the gay center and the librarian going to the locked stacks to get my requested book on 'homosexuality'" (*Making Invisible* 9). Giagni's experience demonstrates how *researching itself* was evidence of the crime of same-sex desire.[6]

In *An Archive of Feeling*, Cvetkovich argues that lesbian archives contrast official libraries and archives because they cultivate emotional rather than strictly intellectual research experiences. But these retroactivists' experiences demonstrate that even official libraries and archives have *always* been emotional for visitors seeking to learn more about their same-sex desire, as LHA and JLMA's collectives were well aware. These grassroots lesbian archive collectives were motivated to provide collections of materials through systems of classification that would cultivate a different experience of lesbian identity: that would counter the pervasive and insidious identification with individual disease and criminality that was stoked by research in official libraries and kept women with same-sex desire from knowing each other present and past. This exigency inspired the organizations' commitment to archival retroactivism as a separatist project, independent from gay-lesbian alliance and the public and academic institutions that had only exacerbated the pain of research.

CLASSIFICATION AS A RHETORICAL *TOPOS*

Systems of classification have had affective and identificatory consequences for women with same-sex desire seeking to learn more about themselves and each other. Yet, in contrast to the injurious research experiences of Martin, Nestle, MacCulloch, and Giagni when they engaged with libraries' materials and arrangement, the rhetoricity of classification has been celebrated from rhetoric's beginnings—as a strategy to break down and discern the parts of the argument. Plato's Socrates, for instance, made the ability to divide and classify central in *Phaedrus*, asserting that "he who is to develop an art of rhetoric must first make a methodological division and acquire a clear impression of each class" (263b). In contemporary rhetorical theory, the classical concern for classification became explicitly connected to identification through Burke, who found identification "clearly apparent in any system of classification" (*Grammar* 417). Through a process of identification, classification functions by *dividing* views and individuals into groups; as Burke explains, identification is "compensatory to division," motivated by dissonance between individuals whose very difference provides the opportunity for rhetoricians to "proclaim their unity" (*Rhetoric* 22).

In drawing Burke's understanding of identification and division into the context of the place-based archive, I emphasize the role of identification in the archive's rhetoricity. Systems of classification in archives draw boundaries around materials, *identifying* records together in distinction from other classificatory categories. As we saw in the Library of Congress's system of classification, materials categorized as "homosexuality" were identified with crime, perversion, and mental illness. Manifesting Burke's concept of identification through division, the system of classification identified materials within the category of homosexuality as a deviation from the norms of heterosexual relations, marriage, nuclear families, and law.

In the context of the history of nonnormative sexuality, Burke's classificatory *identification* becomes the foundation for sexual *identity*. As Foucault has argued, classification has itself been persuasive in encouraging the categorization of individuals into sexual identities. Foucault contends that the latter part of the nineteenth century marked a pivotal moment in the production of homosexuality as a category constituted by a distinct group of people in Western society. The category of homosexuality was produced through medical classification ("sciencia sexualis") to regulate and treat as illness what had previously been considered discrete acts of transgression. The classification of homosexual acts as an enduring disease made an argument for the nature and treatment of queer people. As Foucault suggests, the creation of a category of homosexuality made possible not only the notions of sexual identity we have today but also the strategic targeting of those who engage in nonnormative sexual practices.

Thus acts of transgression become categorized into an enduring quality attached to and eventually internalized by individuals, identifying them together across other "complex and contradictory identifications" (Davis 127) into a shared "substance" of sexual identity. The history of sexuality according to Foucault demonstrates how classificatory categories have identified individuals in terms of pathology, rhetorically shaping sexual identity based on a shared "substance" of disease and malfeasance.

This, as I have explained, is the context in which grassroots lesbian archives like LHA and JLMA set out to intervene with their retroactivism. By creating a different system of classification for selecting and arranging materials from the past, they hoped to shape a different kind of lesbian identity. I suggest that we come to view LHA and JLMA's alternative classification schemas—their approach to the identification/division relation—as a *topos.* Miller defines a *topos* "as a region that permits or invites connection between the abstract and the concrete, between a pattern and the material in which it is instantiated, between *eidos* [form] and *hyle* [matter]" ("Aristotelian Topos" 142). This understanding of *topoi* is an extension of Aristotle's, for whom *topoi* were both constraining and inventional. By aiding in the recognition of relationships among ideas, *topoi* such as definition, division, or comparison serve as a heuristic for generating something new to say or know about a subject. Reconceiving classification as a *topos* accentuates the inextricability of the *pattern* (the system of classification) and the *material* (the artifacts and records themselves) and illuminates how archival classification in certain kinds of material space can encourage certain kinds of unanticipated patterns and connections for visitors.

In LHA and JLMA, the classificatory *topos* encourages visitors to find patterns and connections across a diverse and eclectic collection of artifacts. Rather than rigidly divide the categories that organize materials with sharp distinctions between the normative and the pathological, LHA's system of classification actually encourages associations between disparate materials. Instead of occurring *through* division, in other words, identification happens *across* divisions, across categories. Reconceiving Burkean classification (the identification/division relation) as a *topos* is a way to materialize Burke: to demonstrate how classificatory patterns interact with archival materials to generate identifications, and ultimately, to reconsider the boundaries of identity. In the following sections of this chapter, I examine how first LHA's and then JLMA's classification *topos* functions to transcend divisions between categories of materials.

FRACTURED RESEARCH, ANALOGICAL ASSOCIATION, AND MATERIAL SYNECDOCHE IN LHA

In response to the pain caused by abnormal psychology texts, LHA sought out and made available unpublished material from ordinary and unknown women with same-sex desire rather than medical treatises or the papers of eminent people. Frequently soliciting contributions in their newsletters, LHA characterized donation and preservation as acts of "rejoicing, reclaiming, and renewing" that were imperative to the formation and survival of a lesbian-identified community. Donation was depicted as a way for ordinary individuals to weave themselves into the community fabric by contributing written, spoken (tape-recorded), photographic, or sartorial artifacts to the collective history housed in the archive. In particular, the archive valued ephemeral donations, such as grassroots publications, unpublished diaries and poems, worn artifacts like T-shirts and buttons, and scraps and clippings from newspapers. The nature of these ordinary, ephemeral acquisitions is quite distinct from official libraries' published matter and traditional archives' papers of important individuals. The archive still collected "mainstream" works by academics, clergy, and doctors, but these writings were positioned as "enemy literature" in the archive (Thistlewaite, "Building" 155) and seem to be the minority in a house full of donated special collections and activist ephemera.

Women seeking information about their sexuality thus find sources in LHA very different from what Martin, Nestle, MacCulloch, and Giagni found in their public libraries: instead of being confronted by evidence of their pathology, visitors are encouraged to identify with the thoughts, lives, and desires of ordinary women. Similarly significant was LHA's pledge to serve the entire community, not just academic researchers. One of LHA's enduring principles stipulates that "all lesbian women must have access to the Archives" and that "no academic, political, or sexual credentials are required to use the collection; race and class must be no barrier for use of or inclusion of the Archives collection" (*LHA Newsletter*, 1996). Unlike traditional archives reserved for professional scholars, LHA has always prided itself on being available to the browsing nonacademic and eschews the common request official archives make for a letter of support from an academic institution for use of the archives.

As I will demonstrate, the *browsing* lay researcher is key to LHA's classification *topos*. After signing a brief form, visitors are given the freedom to rifle through the boxes without direct archivist supervision. Like the Sexual Minorities Archive as described by Rawson, LHA too espouses a "logic [that] is a queer imagining of a new historiographic method of archival research, one that carefully accounts for a researcher's body moving through the space of the archives" ("Archiving Transgender" 138). Anyone who has researched in official archives such as university or government collections will note the clear difference between this permission to browse and the more common protocol in which an archivist brings one box or folder at a time to a closely surveilled reading room, removing and restocking it before bringing out another. By contrast, LHA's limestone Brooklyn home (which they purchased in 1992 with money raised from the community) contains couches, a kitchen, and boxes, books, clothing, and more spilling out of every surface, closet, nook, and cranny.

The freedom and practice of browsing are intimately related to the classification schema that organizes the archives' holdings and guides the researcher's journey through the space. Opposing schemas like that of the Library of Congress, LHA resists classificatory procedures that would prescribe and exclude people, orientations, and practices that do not fit in normative categories. As Nestle declared in LHA's 1981 newsletter, "what we call history becomes history and since this is a naming time, we must be on guard against our own class prejudices and discomforts." Nestle's words suggest that LHA's approach to classification in that "naming time" worked against schemas that would exclude or pigeonhole on the basis of prejudice and discomfort. Nestle understood prescriptive, rather than descriptive, selection and arrangement to be implicated with "those who make history the home of the powerful and the prechosen" (*LHA Newsletter* 1984). Connecting "naming" in archival classification with nonprescriptive sexual identity then, Nestle pledged that the archive would "sacrifice no one to the abstract concept of what a lesbian should be" (*LHA Newsletter* 1984); that is, no single understanding of sexual identity would be shored up by narrow and discriminative categories in the archive.

Combating "abstract concepts" and "naming" is a significant challenge in an archive, of course, because archives are arranged in defined categories to facilitate the imagined public's investigations—and this is where *topoi*'s connection between patterns and materials becomes illuminating. Artifacts are filed according to what is judged to be primary (such as author, subject, or medium) and, in the process, distinguished from and grouped with other artifacts in the collection. The patterns set out in finding aids and material juxtaposition guide researchers to particular materials and direct archivists' decisions as they continue to receive and file new holdings.

At first glance, LHA appears to resist naming by doing little in the way of neat classification. The distinctions between materials—that integral part of the identification/division coin of classification—are from the outset compromised. Kate Davy's description of her experience researching the WOW theater group in LHA is telling. After she was directed toward relevant boxes in a general area of the archive, Davy found that

> [i]nto these boxes had been tossed, in no particular order, press releases, programs, scripts, copies of opening night reviews, videotapes of some productions, and a smattering of photographs. Archival work in my case resembled more of an archaeological dig—mining memories and boxes of stuff, carefully examining disparate bits and pieces of a whole, widely scattered and deeply buried. (130)

In LHA the collections are cluttered and jumbled, with boxes and photos spilling out of closets, piled in the corners of hallways and in the middle and edges of rooms. Researchers must unearth and draw connections between "widely scattered and deeply buried" scraps (Davy 130). This is not an archive characterized by clearly marked and defined boxes and folders, with consistently ordered and labeled contents. In fact, while researching in the archive, it is not uncommon to witness a volunteer sorting through existing boxes, occasionally moving and refiling its contents to somewhere else she deems more appropriate.

While the overwhelming array of "tossed" materials could be dismissed as a consequence of an ever-revolving and time-strapped volunteer staff with limited financial resources, I suggest that LHA's collections are organized in a classification schema that *purposively* encourages the bringing together of unlike elements through analogical association. The archive's *topos* fosters what Susan Delagrange describes as the "discovery of affinity and meaning among disparate things." Archivettes generate this affinity and meaning through material rhetorical devices of fractured research, analogical association, and synecdoche. These devices encourage visitors to draw connections between the artifacts and papers, their donors, and the archive's visitors—blurring the boundaries between classificatory categories and queering the sense of lesbian identity with which visitors experience and potentially identify.

Fractured Research and Queer Identity

As Davy suggests, the archive's system of classification actually fractures researchers' ability to search for the totality of a single subject or individual, prohibiting a direct avenue to the object of research and encouraging the careful examination of dispersed bits and pieces.

Despite their seeming disarray, items in the collection are organized through two major categories: by the medium of an artifact and by its content.

Medium-Specific	Content-Specific
Audio/spoken word	Archival
Books	Biographical
Posters (e.g., political events, marches, rallies, literary events, pride events)	Conferences
T-shirts and other multiformatted ephemera	Geographical
	Organizations
	Special collections
	Subjects

Within the *medium-specific* collections, researchers will find materials grouped in categories such as "Audio/spoken Word" (cassette tapes containing recordings of oral histories, diaries, and speeches) and, within such medium-specific categories, some materials are organized under subcategories. Within the *content-specific* collection are subcategories such as "Archival," for information about LHA itself; "Organizations," for activist collectives; "Special Collections," for unsolicited donations; and "Subjects," like domestic abuse or lesbian motherhood.

The rhetorical effect of this *topos*—this pattern and its instantiation in the material—is an exploratory, haptic research experience. The classification schema forces visitors to see, read, touch, and draw connections between far more than the narrow category they may be searching for. Taking my own experience as an example, searching for the Daughters of Bilitis in LHA necessitated digging through far more categories than merely *Organizations.* While this category does contain a large amount of information about the Daughters of Bilitis, so too do the categories of *Conferences* (as they founded, ran, or participated in many), each of which could alternately be filed *Geographically* by the location of the conference. Likewise, an individual Daughter who might be represented in a *Special* collection or *Biographical* file might also be an important proponent of a *Subject* like lesbian motherhood or employment rights, about which they might have published a *Book* or spoken on a tape in *Audio/Spoken Word.* Researchers and visitors following these traces and trails are encouraged by the schema to engage with, and associate, a broader and more abundant array of tangible lesbian artifacts.

The encouragement of cross-categorical association helps to break down the distinctions between classificatory categories, which helps to expand the definition of lesbian beyond prefigured bounds. In Miller's terms, the *topos* of classification is a "conceptual space without fully specified or specifiable contents; it is a region of productive uncertainty" ("Aristotelian" 141). As I searched for the Daughters of Bilitis—a 1950s organization sometimes critiqued for conforming to mainstream social mores—I found myself tracing cofounder Del Martin in the *Subject* files, where I stumbled on adjacent files for transgender men in the media. Martin had no obvious connection to contemporary transmen like Chaz Bono, but the experience of finding these two individuals in the same drawer—even the same archive—demonstrates the queerness of LHA's classificatory approach, the "productive uncertainty" it generates in the relations between "unspecifiable contents" (Miller, "Aristotelian" 141). It is a bold move—one likely to be challenged by transgender advocates and lesbian activists alike—to include a transman in a lesbian archive at all, for Bono is male-identified and straight (though he came out publicly as a lesbian in 1995 prior to his transition). Yet I suggest that Bono's inclusion alongside Martin makes an argument for an ever more inclusive and fluid sense of sexual identity. In this cross-categorical, exploratory research process, researchers like me are compelled to find affinity between seemingly incongruous lives and records and the freedom to browse means that we may at any moment remove materials from different folders and physically lay them down beside one another. The archive's claim to house "lesbian herstory" colors each item in the collections with the identity of lesbian, forcing visitors to expand what that means to accommodate serendipitous incongruities.

While the presence of trans and bisexual materials aids in this expansion of lesbian identity, it also points to some lines in the sand that LHA draws around its expansive diversity. The classification system speaks to the archive's position on transgender: the category sits in the Subject Files, which situates it as a topic of relevance to lesbians that may only fill a folder or few with copies of news clippings, event programs, and other papers. LHA's guide to the subject files on their website asks visitors to "think of these files as 'Lesbians and . . .' The first file is 'Abortion' and the last is 'Youth,'" which suggests some degree of distance between their understanding of lesbian and the topics housed in the Subject files. On this matter, Thistlewaite has written about LHA's mid-1990s decision to include in the collection evidence "relevant" to "all self-identified lesbian lives" ("Building" 163), including current or previously identified lesbians who have transitioned to a male presentation or from male to female. But, perhaps controversially, self-identified men (including trans and cisgender straight and gay men) are not welcome during specifically "women only" hours at the archive, when LHA provides a safe space for forging lesbian-woman identity (Thistlewaite, "Building" 163). These decisions speak to the difficulty of defining and *preserving* sexual and gender identity in an archive, when—as in the case of Chaz Bono—they may change over time.

Indeed, even when gender and sexual identity endures, defining it remains a fundamental problem in doing lesbian history research, when there is rarely, if ever, "ironclad" proof of a "physical, sexually intimate relationship" with another woman (Schwarz, "Researching" 56). Proof of sexual intimacy is not required according to LHA's 1996 published principle, which decrees that "every woman who has had the courage to touch *or desire* another woman deserved to be remembered here" (*LHA Newsletter* 1996; my emphasis).[7] Archivette Judith Schwarz decided that she did not require that a "woman who loves and cherishes another woman as her primary romantic attachment must have sexual contact with her before" calling her a "woman-loving-woman—a lesbian sister" (56). She was more interested in unearthing the history of women who lived their lives outside the "standard protection and more accepted social position of a male-female relationship" than rigidly circumscribing what determines a lesbian ("Researching" 55).

Thus many materials are *produced* as lesbian by nature of their inclusion and placement in this "lesbian herstory" archive. Consider this clipping from a 1976 San Francisco newspaper, which LHA republished in their seventh newsletter:

> BOAT RIDERS WITNESS WOMAN'S DEATH: As more than 100 tourists on a pleasure boat watched, a young woman plunged to her death from the Golden Gate Bridge into San Francisco Bay. . . . Bridge authorities said the unidentified woman carried a box containing the cremated ashes of a former female roommate.

In the newsletter, LHA positions this clipping as evidence of the ways lesbian relationships are euphemized in the mainstream press, revealed only in ambiguous hints, and thus represents the kinds of scraps in which lesbian history is found.

Though researchers may find "more than they are looking for" (Davy 130) through this system of classification that draws connections across disparate materials, they can also find less. Digitized archives and finding aids at other archives are designed to facilitate ease and efficiency for the researcher, with the goal of helping her find precisely (or something close to) what she is looking for. But because most of LHA's holdings are not digitally catalogued (and visitors don't have access to the archive's computer system), the dispersed classification of the massive collection of artifacts and records leaves researchers with the pleasure of discovery but also the inexorable gaps, the "painful erasures . . . from the inevitable, ongoing process of forgetting" (Davy 130). Yet the presence of absence too is rhetorical. The gaps and fissures in an archive of sexuality are fitting; as Cvetkovich explains, lesbian experience, love, desire, and activist organizing are "difficult to chronicle through the materials of a traditional archive" ("In the Archives" 110). When researchers come to LHA and fail to find the totality of a lesbian life and instead find traces of many incongruous lives, drawing connections between them as they cross-categorically dig, a sense of community and the unknowable is reinforced, even if at the expense of the certainty of an individual. Through LHA's system of classification, lesbian identity comes to be defined precisely by this fluid, fractured, at times contradictory collectivity.

Analogical Association and Displayed Artifacts

From the moment visitors enter the archive, it becomes clear that LHA is not a traditional archive with the entirety of the collection neatly concealed in boxes and folders on inaccessible shelves and storage units. Instead, while much of its contents do reside in boxes and folders, the house is "part library, part museum, a community gathering space" ("Lesbian Herstory Archives: Virtual Tour"), littered with objects strategically pulled for display. Buttons and jackets hang in the bathrooms, for example, while photos, book covers, and protest signs are set out on tables and shelves in the main rooms.

Like the connections researchers draw between incongruous categories and lives as we dig through the archive, these displayed artifacts similarly invite visitors to seek affinity between them and with them. As Delagrange maintains, material analogy makes claims for similarity between unlike elements through physical proximity—suggesting that knowledge of one element might help one understand the less familiar other nearby. Rather than reinforce distinct boundaries between categories in the archive, then, the physical proximity of eclectically displayed objects breaks them down.

In their adjacent display, these objects become identified with one another, and when the objects are perceived to represent different, even contradictory factions of lesbian sexuality, the effect is a queering of lesbian identity. As one example of how analogical association functions in the archive to queer identity, consider this pair of boots worn by a parade marshal in at least ten New York City Dyke Marches set adjacent to a bookcase containing pulp fiction from the 1940s and 1950s (figure 2.3). At the time this photo was taken, the boots and books were prominently displayed in the archive's dining room, which often acts a social hub for visitors and archivettes, since it opens to the main reading room and contains the central work area for collective members. Their proximate juxtaposition suggests that the boots are "like" the pulps in some way—in spite of the difference in gender aesthetics, function, and time period. The material arrangement invites associative analogy, the drawing of similarity across the difference of the painted, feminine white women on the covers of the paperbacks and the masculine, ironically patriotic boots worn by marshal Christine McNight. Through the analogical association between various ways that a "lesbian" might "look" (what she might wear, how she might be illustrated), the category of lesbian expands and diversifies. The juxtaposition of seemingly unlike objects disrupts neat classification. Instead of *divisio*, the classification *topos* provokes analogical association between disparate elements and gender aesthetics.

Beyond diversifying gender aesthetics, the boots and books' juxtaposition suggests a unified, if incongruous, tale of lesbian history. While Dyke March parade boots suggest a history of resilience and celebration, the

Fig. 2.3. Boots worn by a marshal of the Dyke March, and pulp fiction paperbacks. *Photo by Saskia Scheffer*

pulps reflect more traumatic experience. In newsletters and LHA's traveling exhibit "Queer Covers," Nestle has dubbed the pulp fiction collection "survival literature." Because these paperbacks were the only representation of lesbianism widely available in the 1940s and 1950s, they were cherished in secret by midcentury women with same-sex desire. But the pulps almost universally punished their lesbian characters with death or heterosexual marriage, and exacerbated stereotypes about same-sex desire as a disease born of desperation for, isolation from, or escape from men. The collocation of these secretly read artifacts of "survival" with a pair of publicly worn pride boots suggests a complex history of trauma and resilience, with which the archive invites lesbian visitors to identify. As Miller explains, *topoi* function this way: as a "conceptual shape or realm where one may find—or create—a detail, a connection, a pattern that was not anticipated deductively by the *topos* itself" ("Aristotelian" 141). The physical arrangement of the books and boots creates the conditions for connections that are not guaranteed or anticipated by the *topos* but are likely to be generated all the same.

The arrangement of displayed objects is, of course, impermanent. At any moment, depending on the whims of an archivette or the uses of the space for different events, the objects may be rearranged, removed, or replaced. But the potential for re-arrangement and re-vision creates the opportunity for ever-new identifications between seemingly incongruous objects and the lives they represent. Despite the potential for ad hoc re-arrangement, the eclectic nature of juxtaposed objects suggests that archivettes endeavor to display particularly diverse materials to increase the potential for similarity-in-difference, for "the discovery of affinity and meaning among disparate things" (Delagrange). This is how *topoi* function—though the materials may change, the patterns of association endure. As Miller explains, following Scott Consigny, the *topos* is both universal and specific, an "instrument with its own capacities that apply to any situation" *and* a "specific place where the rhetor thinks and acts" ("Aristotelian" 141); the *topos* is the pattern (resilience and trauma, masculine and feminine) and its material instantiation (the boots, the books) that together incite connections across difference.

While other archives, of course, contain objects that sit alongside one another, LHA's practice of collecting and displaying visibly *worn* artifacts intensifies visitors' identification with the lives they represent. It is no accident that the archive takes special care to collect clothing and other used or made objects, including

> stickers, buttons, banners from marches, military uniforms, a feather boa, a leather jacket from the Dyketones, an assortment of hats, pasties donated by a lesbian stripper, board games like Lesbian Trivia, rainbow flags and Frisbees, fencing equipment, calendars and date books, roller skates, sculptures and collages. ("Lesbian Herstory Archives: Virtual Tour")

These worn, used, or handmade artifacts suggest *bodies:* active, flesh-and-blood bodies that help bring to life a sense of dynamic lesbian history that itself depends on bodies—on the womanness, desire, and emotion that is the stuff of lesbian experience. Possessions, like the pulp paperbacks donated by Mabel Hampton, a dearly beloved (now deceased) member of the LHA collective, and the boots donated by the Dyke March marshal, contain the traces of their donors and their donors' worlds. Collections of archival objects like these can "connect and include us with others . . . across time and place" (Noble 242), drawing affinity between contemporary visitors, older artifacts, and their previous owners. These objects are meant to be picked up and touched, the tangible evidence of their use felt in the worn creases of the leather boots and the dog-eared pages of marginalia in the pulps. The donors are made real, *felt* to be real, intensifying visitors' identification with the lesbian identities the objects reflect. As Desiree Yael Vester, a longtime LHA volunteer explains, "some [visitors] come here in search of themselves. They just want to touch books that lesbians have held and owned" (qtd. in M. Cohen 9). The sense of community constructed through the material juxtaposition of these worn objects helps sediment, for the visitors who see and touch them, the historical reality of the figures who owned and used them.

The kinds of "records" in this archive then, are clearly different from the deviant categories in official libraries that encouraged pathological identifications in visitors like the DOB, LHA, and JLMA coordinators. Though the pulps' narratives reflect similar accusations of deviance as the library's abnormal psychology texts and system of classification, they are reframed by Nestle's frequent description of them as "survival" literature and their placement next to pride boots. Musing on the "strange act of defiance of [clipping and] filing" bigoted sources, Nestle has written that the placement of pathologizing sources in the "context of our own historical story" helps to "take the sting out of their assumed power" (*LHA Newsletter* 2004). The worn materiality of displayed artifacts (the faded pages, the creases in the leather) is as much a "text" to be read by visitors as the content of the pages, and perhaps more so since visitors rarely pick up a paperback and read it in its entirety during their perusal of the house. These artifacts suggest lives, not diagnoses, and through provoking analogical association among those lives and the life of the visitor, the artifacts expand the definition of lesbian.

Synecdoche and Repetition

Like analogical association, synecdoche operates in the archive to blur the boundaries between classificatory categories. Synecdoche typically refers to a figure of speech where a part is made to stand for the whole, as when a "hired hand" represents a worker. To refigure synecdoche as a *material* rhetorical device, I use the term to denote a relationship between artifacts wherein one object is made to represent the whole collection. In LHA, an artifact becomes synecdochic when it comes to stand for LHA itself, spanning several subcategories at once in the system of classification. I maintain that synecdoche functions in an archive when one artifact is made significant and prominent by *repeating* in various forms and classificatory categories throughout the collection.

A particularly meaningful example of synecdoche is a love letter from a collection of papers once belonging to Eleanor Coit, an early twentieth-century labor activist. After Coit passed away, her family disposed of boxes of letters, wills, leases, and photographs revealing romantic same-sex relationships she had had in her life. A friend of the archive found the boxes on the street and brought them to LHA for safekeeping and preservation. One particular love letter, dubbed the "Gutter Letter" by the archive collective, is synecdochic for LHA because it represents how so much of lesbian history has been tossed away as trash. The letter is a symbol of the archive's exigency and mission to rescue the scraps of lesbian lives from gutters and dumpsters. The Gutter Letter's history of familial shame and disposal also comes to represent something quintessential about the archive's understanding of lesbian experience and identity. Like the Gutter Letter, lesbian lives were thrown away, expelled from disapproving families before finding a sense of "home" in LHA. In this way, the letter synecdochically comes to represent the whole of lesbian identity defined by the archive, serving as a cohering factor in the face of the incongruity and diversity I've described.

The original letter is not synecdochic on its own. Rather, it becomes so through its duplication and repetition in many places throughout the archive's system of classification. The original letter is kept in Coit's files, which are a *Special Collection.* But the letter also reappears in other prominent locations: it is featured in a 1981 LHA newsletter, which is housed in the archive in a binder alongside other newsletters. The newsletter reprinted the letter, couching it in the circumstances of its acquisition and "emphasiz[ing] the reality that the documents testifying to our love are too often considered garbage, destroyed by dismissing or frightened families" (*LHA Newsletter* 1981). Its reprinting in the newsletter makes the letter both about Coit and about the *archive,* since the newsletter binder is the one of first places visitors go to learn about the archive itself, not just its contents. Because the letter spans categories—existing both in Coit's special collection and the newsletters—the synecdochic letter breaks down the separation between archival categories, no longer representative of itself alone but several categories simultaneously.

Further breaking down classificatory categories and contributing to its more universal representation of the archive's mission, the letter repeats again in LHA's long-running slide show. Beginning in 1975, the traveling slide show was a multimodal presentation shown to audiences around the country. Nestle explains that the letter was read aloud against a backdrop of "arresting images" of Coit to tell "another national story about lesbian lives," because Coit's historical moment of the 1920s and 1930s saw the "height of pathologizing of homosexual women and yet here we had another voice, from within the lesbian world, claiming the life affirming power of this love" (Nestle, correspondence). Here Nestle poses the letter in explicit opposition to the deviant categories in traditional libraries and archives, standing for the mission of the archive and the lives it represents and providing a counternarrative of sweet love to the national story of homosexual pathology.[8]

Like the letter, LHA suggests, women with same-sex desire have been shamed and discarded before finding community and home in the archive. This history of trauma, represented and reinforced by the Gutter Letter's synecdoche, functions to provide some coherence to the eclectic and fractured lesbian identity housed in the archive; as a newsletter proclaims, "since the destruction of Sappho's poetry, our herstory has issued a warning that we are among the disinherited." The sense of welcome and rescue that LHA has provided the Gutter Letter, all of the archive's donors, and its diverse visitors colors each of the archive's eclectic holdings, offering an open invitation of identification to visitors whose race, class, subculture, nationality, and even sexual orientation and gender identity might diverge and even conflict. Donors and visitors are brought together in all of their complexity through a shared history of "disinheritance."

Browsing across the Topos *of Classification: Possibilities and Limits*

Each of these rhetorical strategies depends on the unique research experience LHA allows and encourages for its researchers. Without the freedom to browse—to sit with papers, clothes, folders, and boxes from any cross-section of the archive, to move through the space to see and touch displayed artifacts and filed records—visitors would not be able to physically set disparate records next to one another and create proximity and connection across the loose categories that arrange LHA's vast and diverse holdings. The classification system is indeed a *topos:* an "aid to pattern recognition" (Miller, "Aristotelian" 142) that generates new ideas and identifications. It is significant that *topos* is a spatial metaphor, a conceptual *place* that a rhetor can visit to invent. The *topos* is a "container or a vessel" (142)—just like an archive—and reconceiving classification in the material archive *as* a *topos* accentuates how the conceptual system of classification that is instantiated in and by the arrangement of physical records aids in invention and identification.

But, as Miller makes clear, the *topos* both generates and constrains. The invention and identification possible to generate from the *topos* are limited by what materials make it into the archive. From its beginnings, LHA has been dedicated to representing racial, ethnic, and class diversity in the archive. However, as Thistlewaite notes, "this politic of diversity, practiced by many post-Stonewall lesbian and gay political groups, inevitably situates its proponents as self-consciously lacking yet accountable for racial and ethnic diversity it idealizes" ("Building" 160). LHA's concern for representing diversity only underscores the whiteness of the early collective and collections. As Thistlewaite explains, the LHA collective was originally largely white and Jewish and the collections donated in the seventies came from participants in New York City lesbian culture and politics—who were also predominantly white. Since then, through the collective's concerted efforts, the governing collective came to include several lesbians of color and the holdings diversified considerably, incorporating black lesbian publications and materials from black lesbian writing, reading, and dance groups. But Thistlewaite maintains that the "whiteness of the archives often signaled and justified the need for and value of ethnic-based lesbian history projects" that could not rely solely on the archive's contents for their work or be spearheaded by the archive's mainly white collective ("Building" 160). The Asian Lesbians of the East Coast collective wrote in LHA's 1984 newsletter that they found many books and materials on or by Asian lesbians in the archives, but they went on to form their own organization and traveling slide show nonetheless ("Building" 162). Likewise, Latina lesbians would find that LHA's extensive collection of periodicals and books rarely included them (Ramos)–perhaps revealing more about lesbian culture than the archive itself, since LHA was quite dedicated to seeking out and cosponsoring lesbian-of-color history projects. As Thistlewaite explains, LHA has "reflected a lesbian community that is predominantly white, while overtly inclusive and ostensibly open to lesbians of all ethnicities" ("Building" 162). Thus, within the archive, the process of generating connections across difference is sometimes limited by the difference within lesbian communities and cultures themselves and the evidence of those cultures that make their way into the physical space.

PHOTOGRAPHIC TRACINGS AND UNIVERSITY ALLIANCE IN JLMA

In many ways, the approach of the June L. Mazer Archives (JLMA) to classification resembles LHA's, perhaps because of their linked origins and exigencies. Like LHA, JLMA collects worn and used ephemera (including grassroots periodicals, buttons, clothes and shoes, and posters) and favors the collections of "everyday" lesbians over the published tomes of "experts." These contents are arranged into media- and content-specific categories similar to those of LHA, including periodicals, photos, books, posters, buttons, special collections, and subject files. Also like LHA, JLMA serves as a community resource and offers visitors some freedom to browse the collections. JLMA's collections too are selected, arranged, and rearranged primarily by volunteer archivists, as the archive has only recently been able to pay its first compensated employee, Los Angeles photographer Angela Brinskele, for her work as director of communications for the archive. But in two important ways, JLMA diverges from LHA's system of classification: the nature of their photographic displays and their relationship to official archives.

First, a counterpoint: In LHA's Brooklyn home, there are photographs from the long through recent past propped on shelves and pinned to the rare expanse of wall not covered by a bookcase. The faces in the images are recognizable as members of the collective to those already familiar with the archive's history; the photos have no context, no caption. They are like family photographs in a family home, with an implicit assumption that the individuals in the photos will be recognizable as part of the community: Mabel Hampton, Edel, Nestle, and other major figures in the archive's history become familiar faces after even a day of researching in the archive. To borrow Michael Warner's words, the photographs are an identificatory address the archive "hope[s] that people will find themselves in" ("Publics" 58). The photographs do not "simply reflect identities formed elsewhere," but instead visitors' recognition of the photos is "one of the ways by which its members' identities are formed and transformed" (Warner, "Publics" 88, 86). When visitors see these photos, they are hailed as a part of the archive's community through the recognition of photographs and artifacts; there is a sense of identification between those "in the know."

Photos function differently in JLMA, though they are even more conspicuously wallpapered on every available surface. Two of JLMA's most cherished collections are of photos, bound and organized by their donors: Ester Frances Bentley's large collage of women's photos, découpaged on a room divider, and MacCulloch's two-volume photo book of her long relationship with Rita Charette. These holdings demonstrate photo records of *relationships* rather than photos of activist organizing or archives collective members, and both photo exhibits seem to exist outside of the archive's main schema of classification.

The Wall of Women and the Mystery of Martha Foster

Ester Bentley (1915–2004) was a lesbian activist, social worker, and educator, and an established member of the lesbian and gay community in Southern California. Though her special collection boxes at JLMA are fairly comprehensive, one of the archive's most prized artifacts is Bentley's wall of photographs (figure 2.4). The wall is a three-panel, accordion-style room divider wallpapered on both sides with dozens of photographs of women, cut mostly from black-and-white snapshots of their faces. The wall is topped by the title "Celebrating the Women in My Life, 1915–200?" and, tucked among the photographs on a panel are the words "Each picture will be the last of a fleeting moment rescued from the past." Some photographs have a date captioned below them, such as '26, '32, '35, and '45, while others are given a name, such as "Gayle." There is even a photo of a nun, captioned "Sister Joan." The women pictured on the wall are rumored by JLMA to be Bentley's ex-lovers, though the nun and the picture of her mother suggest that more than romantic relationships are represented.

As an archival artifact, the wall of women is curious, for what does it really capture and preserve for visitors? There is little information provided beyond the snapshots and the occasional first name or date. But, while we may learn little from the wall about Ester Bentley except that she lived a long life full of diverse relationships with other women, the wall has indeed served as "connective tissue" for other parts of the collection, as UCLA graduate student and archival volunteer Stacy Wood found (Sher 19–21). Wood was helping to process different parts of the JLMA holdings, including the special collection of one Martha Foster, whose box contained some poetry and hundreds of beautiful photographs taken in approximately the 1930s. In the images, Foster appears in a backyard of a house in the Echo Park neighborhood of Los Angeles, dressed up in glamorous costumes of gowns and jewelry. But besides the gorgeous

Fig. 2.4. "Celebrating the Women in My Life, 1915–200?"; collage on screen, created by Ester Bentley. *Ester Bentley Papers, JLMA. Photo by Angela Brinskele*

black-and-white photos of Foster, little more could be found about her. Wood and Brinskele could not track down a birth or death certificate or an obituary. Finding an old letter with an address on it in her collection, Wood went so far as to visit Foster's Echo Park home with the hopes that a family member might still live there. This was a dead end too.

But it was Ester Bentley's wall that provided a new insight, however tenuous, into Foster. As Wood continued to process parts of the collection and perused Bentley's wall, she was shocked to find a picture of a much older Martha Foster. Foster, it appeared, was a potential ex-lover of Bentley. This clue led Wood to Bentley's own boxes, where she found an old ID card of Martha's and even tax evidence that Bentley and Foster had shared a home (Sher). These traces do not reveal when the two women were in a relationship or for how long. Yet the connection is significant, because there appears to be no other evidence of Foster in city archives or online. Her memory seems to exist solely in this archive and, even then, in relation to Bentley and in her costumed photographs.

The Bentley-Foster connection itself, rather than solving the mystery of Martha Foster, only raises more questions. As Wood explains, Bentley's collections are relatively comprehensive and there is so much known about this woman through her deep involvement in community organizing and activism. Bentley's photograph of Foster showed her in middle age. If so much was known about Ester Bentley, how could so little be known about her live-in lover? If they shared a house, how could Bentley herself provide no more than a snapshot and an old ID card? How could Foster have no ties to the many organizations and affiliations that Bentley was involved in?

Bentley's wall, then, only seems to stand alone, outside the classification schema of the collection. The room divider stands upright in the space between the periodical collections and the subject file cabinets at JLMA. Though donated by Bentley, it is not kept with her special collection boxes, since its size and shape far exceed an archival box and its value to the archive keeps it centrally displayed. But the wall serves as "connective tissue," as Wood put it, between the traces of lives that are represented in the archive (qtd. in Sher 19). Bentley's wall hints at relationships and connections while reminding us of our inability to pin them down and know them. Thus the photographs can suggest a history of intimacy and connection—which is powerful and in many ways the purpose of archival retroactivism—but they stop short of the assurances of existence offered by the factual records (like birth, death, and tax documentation) typical of official archives.

The "connective tissue" that photographs become in JLMA are not limited to Bentley's collage of lovers. In a JLMA thirty-second-anniversary video, board member Jamey Fitzpatrick describes her experience showing photographs to visitors of the archive:

> I'll see a picture and be showing it to somebody as a part of a tour and a woman will say, "oh wait, there's Sally in the background" or, you know, "I was right over the side there helping lift something out of the truck." And for a moment that history comes alive and you can see how excited people are to see their own life histories within our walls. (Mazerarchives)

The photographs as connective tissue contribute to the archive's retroactivism. They provide evidence of connection across time and place and, as Bentley's wall suggests, the prospect of having a full, varied, long life of lovers, family, and friends.

A Relationship in Photos

Nancy "Bunny" MacCulloch, who brought the West Coast Lesbian Collections to Los Angeles with Mazer, was meticulous in documenting her own love life. While her special collection boxes contain several folders of writings and memorabilia from her life, two photo albums sit outside the collection like Ester's wall of ex-girlfriends. The photo albums are housed on shelves in the archive's audio-video room—an outlier outside the system of classification. These albums document her relationship with Rita Charette from 1955 to their 1965 breakup, and then again from 1974 when they reunited.

The photos and captions are snapshots of these women's relationship and their experiences together. Many of the photos are of the everyday: for instance, a photo of a smiling MacCulloch hanging her undergarments on a drying rack is captioned (likely by Charette), "Nancy and her damned eternal clean underwear," while a photo of the couple smiling wearily with friends is captioned, ". . . hungover." The photos also document the couple's holidays and trips: the young women in front of a Christmas tree, a six-week trip to a Grand Canyon cabin, a week in a Cape Cod cottage. There are pictures of the couple with friends in their apartment in costumes or at Venice Beach in winter.

But these are settings and scenes and not quite what the photographs capture. There is a spirit in the photos and captions, a youthful liveliness and independence that can be gleaned from the witty captions and playful actions depicted in the images. For example, a picture of Charette dressed up and preening in a garden is captioned, "Rita practices looking lovely for trip to San Francisco," with the next picture captioned, "And so does

Bunny." The many road trips and the visible laughter, parties, and friends offer traces of this couple's energetic independence and public same-sex relationship in a time when being out in public was socially and physically dangerous. So do their occupations and entrepreneurship. Charette is photographed in her WAC training battalion uniform on the army base in 1959, while other photos capture her building her first radio for the military. MacCulloch is photographed editing film (her occupation for much of her life), and a note in the album reveals that Charette and MacCulloch bought a laundromat business in 1963 called the "Why Not Wash."

While Bentley's wall of women suggested webs of connections across the archive and beyond, illustrating her long, full life of varied love, MacCulloch's photo albums suggest for lay researchers the potential for the longevity of one relationship. After documenting ten years of their relationship, the first album ends in 1965 with a note that says, "We split up in late April 1965—but not end of story! See volume 2 which starts 1974." The albums provide visible evidence of a lasting love that nonetheless ran its course sometime before 1979, when MacCulloch began seeing Mazer. Taken together—as most visitors to the archive would, since MacCulloch's albums and Bentley's wall are likely staples of any archive tour—the collections of the photos demonstrate the fullness and longevity of lesbian love, even when it ends. There is something intangible captured in these photo collections that can only be described as traces of relationships, connections drawn across, within, and outside of categories in the archive.

Institutional Alliance and the Topos *of Classification*

Before concluding this chapter, I want to emphasize briefly how significant grassroots lesbian archives' instantiation in homes and community is to the *topos* of classification and the dynamic, flexible sense of lesbian identity and history the *topos* encourages. This significance becomes clear after JLMA's recent alliance with a major public institution.

First, another counterpoint: LHA has from the beginning been deeply committed to their independence from public and academic institutional involvement. The archive's holdings would be housed in its home or off-site storage facilities but never "bartered or sold" to academic or other public institutions. The principle came first from a distrust of those institutions, which had caused much pain in individuals seeking to learn more about their same-sex desire. LHA's distrust of public institutions was a product of the context of its origins in the 1970s era of liberation.

Its founders had experienced the police raids on queer public space that continued from the 1950s through the 1970s; they were witnesses to police violence against antiwar and civil rights protests and the Stonewall riots; they had lived through the McCarthy era's purges and violent suspicion. All of these recent historical and lived experiences influenced the broader ethos of liberation and the specific politics of LHA. As Nestle wrote in 1979, "to ask the patriarchal destroyer to preserve is a suicidal act. It does not express our sinister wisdom. We would be surviving in their context, in an ongoing world dedicated to power, elitism, and survival of the patriarchal fittest" ("Notes on Radical Archiving," 10).

So the archive had to be protected *from* these public institutions, not handed over to them. And despite being an archive, it was constructed not to create easier access and more systematically classified collections for academic experts but instead to provide a safe, historical space for lesbian visitors. In fact, in 1979, the archive was granted the legal status of an incorporated nonprofit educational foundation, rather than the more strictly regulated definition of archives and libraries (Thistlewaite, "Building" 160). The keepers of the archive then began to hold "At Home at the Archive" events with music, talks, readings, and other activities, and continued their work traveling to bars, homes, churches, and festivals to present slide shows of the archive's holdings and to solicit donations of documents and artifacts from attendees.

While JLMA has espoused a similar emphasis on community involvement, its caretakers have been less rigid about their alliance with public institutions. Recently, many of the archive's holdings were moved to a major state research university, the University of California Los Angeles (UCLA). In 2007 the UCLA Center for the Study of Women (CSW) received a two-year grant to process and digitize five of JLMA's larger collections through a project they called Access Mazer; after the success of this arrangement, UCLA's CSW received a grant from the National Endowment for the Humanities to "formalize a collection building and preservation partnership" (*Making Invisible* 23). JLMA was interested in the alliance because it had run out of room for new materials in its West Hollywood space and two off-site garages. Like LHA, however, JLMA was wary of ceding ownership of the materials to a major public institution. While they trusted UCLA's Center for the Study of Women, which had long focused on Los Angeles–area women's and lesbian organizations, they could not be sure that UCLA would not change their principles and values

(*Making Invisible* 14). Over time, however, UCLA and JLMA negotiated a unique contract whereby UCLA's archives would hold the materials but JLMA would maintain ownership of them. JLMA "had an organizational crisis" over the decision, board president Ann Giagni admits, but believed that their very legacy as a community-based, grassroots organization would continue to encourage lesbians to donate their "everyday" materials to JLMA (*Making Invisible* 20). The agreement with UCLA stipulated that JLMA could take the materials back if they were ever moved from Los Angeles or sat unprocessed and unavailable for too long.

JLMA's *topos* changes considerably in this arrangement. While the small West Hollywood space remains full and vibrant—with shelves packed with boxes and books, walls covered in photos, and volunteers chatting and filing—many of their larger collections (including both MacCulloch and Mazer's) now require a trip to UCLA's Charles E. Young Research Library's Special Collections department. This basement room is strictly monitored. When I visited the special collections to view materials belonging to JLMA, an administrator guarded the locked door and buzzed me in after I had locked all of my belongings outside in a locker and specified which two boxes I would be permitted to peruse that day. Inside the cold, silent room, another administrator would go to a concealed area and bring me one small box at a time.

Because visitors are not permitted to browse in this space but instead are limited to one box (which may only have a few folders in it) at a time, the sense of cross-categorical association is limited. Instead of sitting among other women, any of whom might be there to research, volunteer, or browse her history, I sat with other academics researching topics such as mathematics. Worn Dyke March boots do not sit next to racy pulp paperbacks in this room; there is no sense that generations of women have touched and associated the belongings of generations more. Thus JLMA currently occupies a hybrid space in which the constraints of their *topos* may come to outweigh its generativeness, even as they benefit from the financial and physical security of the academic institution.

CONCLUSION

Grassroots lesbian archives have operated through a *topos* of classification that encourages cross-categorical associations and an expansive understanding of lesbian identity for the browsing researcher. Through the *topos*, the archives wield rhetorical strategies for drawing those connections between disparate materials, including fractured research, analogical association between displayed artifacts, and synecdoche as key materials "repeat" across the collection in a variety of classificatory categories. JLMA also demonstrates how photographic holdings, like MacCulloch's decades-long relationship albums and Bentley's large "wall of lovers," can stand outside the classification system of the collection, nonetheless serving as connective tissue across the gaps in the collection's historical record. These strategies help the archives encompass and encourage a multivalent, fluid lesbian identity that opens itself to the unwieldy inclusion of bisexual, trans, and racially diverse materials.

These archives' rhetoricity is, finally, clearest in the fissures in their plenitude, when what they do *not* preserve becomes visible. In LHA's political and identificatory objective of inclusivity, there is evidence of absence—the absence of the conflict that likely exists in such a diverse archive and collective. In searching for the making of a 1987 documentary film about the Daughters of Bilitis, which was to be produced jointly by LHA and Morgan Gwenwald, Manuela Soares, and Sara Yager, I found dozens of hours of raw audio and film footage of interviews with former DOB members from across the country; entire boxes of correspondence, scripts, and notes; and flyer evidence of work-in-progress screenings—but somehow the archive possessed no finished film. I continued to dig cross-categorically through the archive, seeking answers for its absence that were not there to be found, an odd development for a video project that had so painstakingly documented itself. Edel, Nestle's cofounder of LHA, eventually informed me that the DOB video project had dissolved, despite hundreds of hours of work, because of issues such as the script, funding, and group dynamics among the filmmakers. The archive did not preserve any evidence of conflict among members of the collective and filmmaking team. The gaps, where conflict might have been but cannot be found, are a part of this queer archive's rhetorical objective of a radical inclusivity that incorporates difference without "having differences." Perhaps the filmmakers elided from record the strife among lesbians revealed by the project's dissolution, protecting themselves and their history from evidence of dissonance.[9]

The next chapter takes up the question of complicity in the composition of lesbian history by examining how archival documents and artifacts are translated and reproduced in new, multimodal compositions of lesbian history. LHA is itself involved in repackaging archival materials outside the archive's walls—through its newsletters, its slide show, the video project that never was. These "remediations" of the archive outside its physical space constitute a kind of rhetorical activity different from archivization. But in their remediation projects, LHA does not make explicit its role in selecting and arranging sources to share publicly. Because its primary medium for composing lesbian history is archivization, LHA cannot undermine the status and authority it wishes to bestow on ordinary lesbians and the ephemera so often tossed away as trash. In contrast, as the next chapter demonstrates, many more recent documentary film- and video makers who employ archival materials in the making of new compositions of lesbian history do grapple with historiography, using different technologies and techniques. These compositions then become a part of the evolving lesbian archive.

3. REMEDIATING THE ARCHIVE

DOCUMENTARY COMPOSITIONS OF LESBIAN PASTS

> With respect for the partially known, the unknown, and the never to be known, the archivist must gingerly embrace the remains and construct what must ultimately be considered fictive stories from the past. —Barbara Hammer, *Hammer!*

> One of the ways that documentary film and video expand the lesbian archive is by documenting the archive itself.
> —Ann Cvetkovich, "In the Archives of Lesbian Feeling"

Twenty years after the Lesbian Herstory Archives (LHA) was established to collect and preserve a vulnerable past, a small, diffuse movement of filmmakers began to extract and reframe archival records in experimental documentaries. While filmmakers such as Barbara Hammer, Cheryl Dunye, Jean Carlomusto, and Su Friedrich were previously known for experimental short films, their compositions grew into feature-length lesbian history films in the 1990s, typically running at least sixty minutes. Others turned to filmmaking anew, including Joan E. Biren, a feminist activist and photographer who directed several documentaries focusing on lesbian activism in the 1990s.[1] These compositions "document the archive itself," as Cvetkovich asserts (251): a meta-archival practice that encourages viewers to reflect on the process of preservation. Hammer describes this process as a "ginger embrace" of the past's remains and the construction of "what must ultimately be considered fictive stories" (263). Her emphasis on the construction and sometimes fabrication of the past in its compositional process is a key feature of the retroactivism of these filmic histories.

Documentary compositions of lesbian history produced in the 1990s move beyond collecting and narrating the past to assaying how—and whether it is even possible—to compose lesbian history. The filmic composers featured in this chapter address critical historiographic questions such as the following: What is the relationship between the archive and the past it represents? What is the role of the retroactivist in the production of queer history as "fictive stories"? How do retroactivists deal with aspects of potentially queer historical figures deemed "unsavory" by contemporary politics? And can retroactivists compose queer history at all, when to "queer" lesbian history may mean challenging the very category of lesbian in the first place?

The films' emphasis on critical historiography departs from earlier forms of retroactivism I have discussed thus far. The LHA and the June L. Mazer Archives, for example, do not overtly distinguish between their archival materials and the pasts the materials trace. Despite the impact of classificatory decisions on how researchers engage the materials, place-based archives tend to treat artifacts and documents *as* the past itself, underplaying archivists' rhetorical choices of selection and arrangement. Because LHA's retroactivist rhetoric depends on their granting "status" to the artifacts and images of lesbians previously judged "unarchivable" (Mbembe 20), LHA was understandably wary about undermining the authority the archive is meant to offer the lives of past and present lesbians by emphasizing the archive's role in the production of those lives. Likewise, Martin and Lyon's archive of anecdotes in *Lesbian/Woman* begins with an assurance that the authors had recalled the experiences from "thousands of women" with whom they had "talked to, counseled, socialized with, and been friends with" over the previous decades (9). The authors frame the anecdotes as the experiences of other women rather than the invention of their pen.

In contrast, the filmic compositions examined in this chapter are overtly and reflexively historiographic, as the composers emphasize their role in making, and challenging, lesbian history. The filmmakers in this chapter disrupt the reliance on both glorified and stigmatized lesbian pasts exhibited by prior generations of retroactivists because if, as Scott Bravmann contends, "accounts of the past themselves help 'make' or 'construct' a fiction of the modern homosexual," then interrupting the archive's bond with reality has the potential to disturb the formation of identifications. These filmic historiographers are motivated to challenge lesbian history because some historical compositions can seem to cement inequality within and between sexually identified communities by circumscribing static or exclusive identifications—something LHA was also concerned about as they actively sought to racially diversify the archive. It is in this way that the films are most rhetorical, for they put pressure on viewers' subconscious dependencies upon lesbian history for present sexual identification.

The strategies employed by the filmmakers to purvey retroactivist historiography are multimodal in order to present, frame, modify, and even invent archival materials.[2] Multimodal strategies makes use of multiple "semiotic modes" such as sound, moving and still images, and performance, with particular attention to the "way in which the modes are combined" (Kress 20). The multimodality of the retroactivist documentary films "remediates" (Bolter and Grusin) archival materials, enfolding and combining modes of text, image, moving image, and sound in filmic compositions.

The reuse of indexical audiovisual media in new filmic compositions reformulates the meaning of "archival document." While in place-based archives like LHA, documents become "archival" by virtue of their selection and preservation in the space called archive, Jaimie Baron suggests that we understand the "archival" status of appropriated audiovisual materials differently. She argues that documents remediated on film and video become archival through an "experience of reception" rather than by their former placement in physical archives; these "archival documents exist as 'archival' only insofar as the viewer of a given film perceives certain documents within that film as coming from another, previous—and primary—context of use or intended use" (Baron 7). This experience of reception refigures the archival nature of found footage into a product of a *relationship* with the viewer—which is to say, the archival document as such emerges in the context of its address and reception. In this chapter, I argue that the appropriation (and, per Baron, invention) of archival documents in filmic compositions of lesbian history affords a meta-archival approach to retroactivism that poses and pursues critical questions of queer historiography in relationship with viewers.

After the context of queer filmmaking, activism, and studies in the 1990s is outlined below, each of five sections that follow couples a conceptual innovation in lesbian filmic historiography with the multimodal rhetorical strategy that facilitates it:

1. *Unstable identity categories:* the representation of fluid identifications and the resistance of historical subjects to being placed in

static, primary, sexually defined categories by historians, employing the multimodal strategy I call "gainsaying." This section focuses on Hammer's *The Female Closet.*

2. *Achronological memory:* the use of memory as historiographic material, employing the multimodal rhetorical strategy of "nonlinearity." This section focuses on Hammer's *Tender Fictions.*

3. *Unapologetic imaging of taboos:* the visible and central role of archival images that are discounted or scorned both within and outside lesbian communities, employing the multimodal rhetorical strategies of imagery and cinematic temporality. This section focuses on Hammer's *Nitrate Kisses.*

4. *Fictitious archives:* the fabrication or obvious manipulation of archival evidence, employing the multimodal rhetorical strategies of appropriation and juxtaposition. This section focuses on Hammer's *History Lessons* and Dunye's *The Watermelon Woman.*

5. *Camp historiography:* the performative exaggeration of iconic lesbian history to simultaneously honor and critique representations of the lesbian past, employing the multimodal rhetorical strategy of "embodied performance." This section focuses on Jean Carlomusto et al.'s *Not Just Passing Through.*

CONTEXTUALIZING QUEER RESISTANCE IN FILMIC HISTORIOGRAPHY

The context in which these multimodal compositions were made informed the composers' historiography—and differs from the rhetorical situations that motivated previous retroactivists. In 1992 film critic B. Ruby Rich heralded the nineties as the era of "new queer cinema" in influential pieces in the *Village Voice* and *Sight and Sound.* She deemed the decade a "watershed" moment for "independent gay and lesbian film and video," citing an unprecedented popularity and prevalence of the films at general and queer film festivals alike (15).[3] Rich noted that while "new queer" films were not identical in their approaches and concerns, they did share a style of "appropriation and pastiche, irony, as well as a reworking of history with social constructionism very much in mind" (16). These attributes are apt descriptions of the strategies purveyed by the filmic historiographers featured in this chapter.

Barbara Hammer, Cheryl Dunye, and Jean Carlomusto and her sister filmmakers are not explicitly named by Rich as a central part of this wave, perhaps because the first of their contributions to lesbian historiography (Hammer's *Nitrate Kisses*) was released shortly after Rich first wrote in the *Village Voice*,[4] and the others appeared later throughout the 1990s. But Rich also provides a second salient reason for their absence that sets some context for the production and reception of lesbian-themed films at these festivals. Reflecting on New Queer Cinema's 1992 advances, Rich asks "what will happen to the lesbian and gay filmmakers who have been making independent films, often in avant-garde traditions, for decades already?"—filmmakers like Hammer, who had been making films on lesbian subjects since the 1970s and often speaks of the influence of avant-garde artists like Maya Deren on her work. Could Hammer be considered "new" queer cinema and, more to the point, could any woman attain the same level of success? "Surprise," Rich writes dryly; "All the new movies being snatched up by distributors, shown in mainstream festivals, booked into theatres, are by the boys" (17). What about Cheryl Dunye? she asks. What about Jean Carlomusto? "Will lesbians ever get the attention for their work that men get for theirs?" Rich wondered (22).

Nonetheless, despite the comparatively lesser attention these filmmakers received that year, their approaches, subjects, and purposes fit well within Rich's New Queer Cinema, expressing what she called a "new kind of lesbian video" and a "contemporary lesbian sensibility" (19). Other qualities of New Queer Cinema, outlined by film scholar Michele Aaron (3–5), include

- focusing not only on lesbian and gay communities but the factions and subcommunities that diversify them;
- "eschewing positive imagery" and remaining "unapologetic" about a character's shortcomings and malfeasance;
- "defying the sanctity of the past" by remixing, reediting, and undermining dominant heterosexual historical narratives; and
- breaking formal conventions with experimental and appropriated techniques.

Within or alongside the emerging wave of New Queer Cinema, the filmmakers featured in this chapter used many of these approaches in their explicitly lesbian-focused historiographic films.

New Queer Cinema did not emerge in a vacuum, of course. Propelled by the devastation of AIDS, direct action groups like ACT-UP (AIDS Coalition to Unleash Power) and Outrage had been organizing across the boundaries of sexual and gender identifications since the late 1980s. Queer studies scholar Douglas Crimp wrote in 1993 that groups like ACT-UP were quintessentially queer, as the fight for proper treatment for AIDS patients drew "identifications across [gender, sexual, and racial] identities" (315). Crimp represents just one voice in the concurrent rise of queer studies in the academy, which was inspired by (in addition to academic influences like Foucault and Butler) the activism of groups like ACT-UP and cultural works such as the films of New Queer Cinema.[5] While these films were being produced, queer theory emerged to destabilize the consolidation of identity labels and politics. Despite the diversity of opinions and prevalence of debate in queer studies, this field largely defined its work initially as the "shared dissent of the dominant organization of sex and gender" (Duggan, *Sex Wars* 157) as binary, naturalized categories (male, female, gay, straight).

Queer studies' "dissent" of normative sex and gender extended to *historical* scholarship that reproduced the logics of liberal tolerance and fixed-identity politics. As Warner explained in 1993, "queer gets a critical edge by defining itself against the normal rather than the heterosexual, and normal includes normal business in the academy": histories that recover gay and lesbian "heroes" without troubling the system of value that determines what hero means, the system that arbitrates what Dana Cloud calls the "good gays." Though Cloud writes more than a decade after Hammer, Dunye, and Carlomusto and colleagues produced their historiographic films, her critique is helpful in contextualizing their rhetorical approach. For Cloud, the "good gays" are the historical figures that "do not challenge mainstream norms of intimate and familial behavior, the rules of capitalist society (to work and consume), and the assumption that one will work within a mainstream political framework" (25).[6] Halberstam explains why "good gay" recovery can hinder present politics: "Focusing excessively on a mythic queer past . . . actually produces a romanticized notion of a gay past . . . and then neutralizes the potency of critiques of that past that emerge in the queer present" ("Shame" 222). For Halberstam and Cloud—and the filmmakers in this chapter—a glorified gay past can obscure the inequalities *within* gay and lesbian histories that persist in the present—exclusions based on age, race, class, gender, and other vectors of difference—which can make it more difficult to challenge them.

The filmmakers examined in this chapter emerge in this context with a hybrid retroactivist stance that both critiques historiographies that operate in the normalizing logic of gay activism and at the same time continues to compose history in hopes of a more equitable, inclusive future. That is, they recognize and represent the challenges, and even impossibility, of making queer lesbian history but continue to look creatively to the past to compose it nonetheless.

The most prolific producer of lesbian historiographic films in the 1990s was Barbara Hammer, who made four such films, including *Nitrate Kisses* (1992), *Tender Fictions* (1996), *The Female Closet* (1997), and *History Lessons* (2000). Hammer suggests her awareness of academic queer studies by quoting Foucault, Cvetkovich, Sue Ellen Case, and other scholars in her films. Still a prolific filmmaker and now a part-time professor of experimental cinema in Switzerland, Hammer is considered the grande dame of lesbian film, having produced her first experimental short film on lesbian subjects in the 1970s. She is known for her humorous experimentation with formal film qualities, using optical printing, superimposition, and digital animation to create faded, overlapping textures and whimsical manipulations of existing media. When she began to make feature-length documentary films about lesbian history in the 1990s, she retained her signature experimental approach characterized by manipulated textures and nonnarrative sequences.

Also examined here is *The Watermelon Woman* (1996), written and directed by and starring Cheryl Dunye, a Liberian-born filmmaker whose work often focuses on black lesbians and black history. Her films are not strictly documentaries but rather what she calls "Dunyementaries," which blur fiction and the historical past by incorporating real and invented archival footage, on-street interviews, and confessional scenes. Dunye's film features cameos from well-known lesbian scholars, such as Sarah Shulman and Alexandra Juhasz (who produced the film). Finally, this chapter also features *Not Just Passing Through* (1994), which focuses on lesbian archives, history, and activism and was directed by Jean Carlomusto, Dolores Perez, Catherine Gund Saalfield, and Polly Thistlewaite. Like Hammer, both Dunye and Carlomusto are now university professors of film and media. Thus these filmmakers sat in a unique position between academic and public history, as they were in conversation with queer studies but produced lesbian historiography for audiences outside the academy.[7]

The rest of this chapter delves into the films themselves, focusing on five specific retroactivist strategies and the rhetorical impact of their historiographic innovations.

DISSENTING IDENTITY CATEGORIES THROUGH "GAINSAYING"

A lineage of lesbian history—and the recovery of historical figures into it—depends on some enduring understanding of "lesbian" that marks and binds figures across time and cultures. But if the stable and consistent categorization of "lesbian" undergirds lesbian history as a concept, what happens when figures resist being defined within its bounds? Given the rhetorical goals of retroactivism, we might expect a retroactivist to sublimate the resistance of the historical figure, or to speak for her, framing her as a lesbian hero in a growing lineage. Hammer, however, takes a different approach, employing a strategy I have called "gainsaying": the representation of a conversational altercation between a historian with a retroactivist agenda and a resistant historical subject. If Hammer's retroactivist project were simply to write a history of a lesbian hero, she might edit out the unruly resistance of her historical subjects in her final composition, but instead she *emphasizes* it so that both her effort to recover a lesbian hero and the figure's resistance are preserved. Gainsaying allows the resistant figure's voice to complicate simplistic "good gay" recovery by refusing to perform the role of a glorified heroine. By recording a dialogic argument, both sides come into view: the political and personal needs of the historian and the divergent desires of the historical figure. Gainsaying becomes multimodal on film and video, which can capture the discursive dialogue and emotional cues of the conflict and conversation.

To illustrate the multimodal strategy of gainsaying, I concentrate on Hammer's 1997 documentary *The Female Closet*, a sixty-minute film featuring three (arguably) lesbian artists. Stylistically, this film is one of Hammer's more traditional documentaries, neatly divided into three biographical sections on artists Nicole Eisenman, Alice Austen, and Hannah Höch. In the interest of space, I focus here on the segments featuring Eisenman, a contemporary artist, and Austen, a nineteenth-century American photographer. From the gainsaying in these segments, viewers witness the acts of making history and naming lesbians as always contested and political. The segments suggest ways viewers might continue to examine and recover historical figures as somehow lesbian while simultaneously resisting the capture of the figures into static and anachronistic identity categories.

Eisenman is an acclaimed New York artist, known for her large-scale murals and canvases which in the 1990s often featured fantastical images of lesbians fighting minotaurs, lesbian superheroes, Amazons capturing and castrating pirates. In the segment, Hammer interviews Eisenman and impels the artist to save her artifacts, her sketches, the records of her life, because "after artists are deceased, if you don't declare your sexuality publicly, museums can say you weren't gay." Here, Hammer-as-interviewer echoes gay historians like Michelangelo Signorile and Larry Gross, who argue that gay men and lesbians in positions of power or fame have a responsibility to declare their sexuality for posterity—to become the heroes of history that challenge stigma for future gay men and lesbians.

Yet Eisenman is unconvinced by Hammer's pressure to preserve and declare her sexuality or risk its loss for future gay and lesbian people. She gainsays with surprise: "Really? You'd think it'd be a good thing [for artists] to say they're gay. I mean, I don't know any artists in the closet. It's too hard to be in the closet as an artist. You don't have much of a choice if you're showing it [in your work]. I'm not getting lower prices because I'm gay." Eisenman is incredulous that any artist would closet herself—or even be able to—because she understands art to be a deeply expressive project; perhaps even more so, Eisenman understands that rebellion has currency in the economy of art. Indeed, she admits that she got her big break during the "lesbian chic" zeitgeist of the nineties. Later in the film, Eisenman shares her history of drug addiction and her cushy Scarsdale upbringing. At each turn, Eisenman rejects Hammer-as-interviewer's attempt to use her success for a present politics of heroic rescue.

Despite the success that she in part attributes to her sexuality, Eisenman resists Hammer's implication that she should be remembered "as a lesbian." Argues Eisenman, "I don't know that the word 'lesbian' pigeonholes an artist, but I don't want to see the totality of an artist's work be about one issue. I don't want to be trapped in any particular category." Hammer repeatedly makes assumptions about what is primary about Eisenman—namely, her sexuality—while Eisenman just as consistently blocks Hammer's attempts to name her. When Hammer pushes on, arguing that the graphic homoerotic scene she films Eisenman painting is "made for lesbians" (implying that Eisenman should identify more strongly as a *lesbian* artist), Eisenman laughs and replies, "Actually, this is for a married woman who wants a lesbian scene on her ceiling. It's erotic for everyone. It just looks good, makes for gorgeous subject matter. Heterosexual collectors buy this stuff up." Eisenman's gainsaying rejects the idea that desire maps neatly onto identity categories, against Hammer's insistence that her work be about and for lesbians.

Eisenman's resistance to Hammer's attempts to categorize her and her viewers in sexual identity categories points to a challenge for queer historiography: the incongruence between queerness (the persistent destabilization of identity and normativity) and sexual-identity-based recovery (the recruitment of historical figures into an enduring identity category). Eisenman gainsays Hammer's retroactivist attempt to position her as a "good gay," a historical heroine trailblazing the way for future lesbian artists. Eisenman even admits that she occasionally "passes" as straight when it conveniences her life. Although she generally considered herself an "out" lesbian, she shares on film, "I tend to make my life easier" by concealing her sexuality in certain situations. Despite the heroic fantasy world of her art, Eisenman makes no claims to be a lesbian heroine herself, only a heroin addict who sometimes passes as straight to avoid unnecessary strife.

Film and video have the capacity to preserve conversation: the emotion, the voices, the body language, and the interchange that happen in historiographic gainsaying. The multimodal nature of film captures Eisenman's voice coming from her own body; it captures Eisenman's surprise and frustration in response to Hammer's pressure in ways that extend beyond language. As much as viewers understand that film, video, and photographs can be manipulated, there is no detectible deception here. The video appears to have caught an unprovoked refusal to participate in the recovery brand of retroactivism.

While Hammer's presence in the film as an assertive interviewer reveals a conviction that lesbian figures should demand historical representation, the film itself represents the *tension* between a present desire to rescue lost history and the historical figure's wishes to be remembered more complexly than by a primary identity category. Hammer does not edit out Eisenman's responses, even though they seem to defy her interviewer's project of recovering and preserving lesbian history. The multimodal nature of film, and Hammer's preemptive recovery of a living artist who can still speak for herself, allows Hammer to argue for conscious efforts to preserve and declare nonnormative sexuality *and* indicate the potential resistance by historical figures to their being remembered solely by this sexuality. She both recovers and undermines the terms that make lesbian recovery possible. The rhetorical significance of this strategy is in the interruption of viewers' own claiming of Eisenman as a lesbian foremother. Viewers are left not with lesbian history but with its slipperiness, its evasion of Hammer's and perhaps their own attempts to claim affinity with a successful artist. The gainsaying represented in the film models the queer historiographic process in which efforts to produce a glorified lineage of a lesbian past come into conflict with the flawed and agential humanity of its historical figures. Hammer disrupts the identificatory potential of a lesbian history containing the vibrant and creative Eisenman.

The filmmaker's decision to show the constraints of identity-based historical rescue and the unruliness of historical figures anticipates queer historiographic cautions about recovery. Taking rumors of Eleanor Roosevelt's same-sex relations as an example, Cloud has critiqued the "logic of outing" historical figures as if their "identities were a knowable, fixed essence" (24). Roosevelt presents a complicated case for recovery into a lesbian history because of both her ambiguous relationship with journalist Lorena Hickok and her difficult but politically expedient relationship with her husband. But Cloud contends that it is precisely Roosevelt's ambiguity that should interest queer historians of rhetoric instead of a need to stabilize her as a lesbian and situate her in lesbian history. Because queer studies understands sexuality identity as a "set of culturally constituted and collectively and individually performed semiotics and behaviors," historians cannot conclude with any assurance that any historical figure is "one of us (whoever we are)," writes Cloud (39). Rather than recover a historical figure within an assumption of an essentialist homosexuality that endures across time and culture, Cloud urges queer historians to instead *queer* historical figures by examining how their private lives trouble "assumptions of heteronormativity" (39). In other words, Cloud suggests that queer historians should inquire into how the figures in fact defy inclusion into prefigured categories.

In Hammer's filmic representation, Eisenman's life and work, like Roosevelt's, suggest a fluid identity, one that shifts in its primary attributes—from artist, to lesbian, to addict, to someone passing as straight—at times conjoining attributes and at others rejecting them entirely. As Cloud argues, "it matters less what someone is than what they and the texts that represent them *do*" to our assumptions about sexuality (40). The multimodal nature of film allows Hammer to record Eisenman's resistance to being posed as a lesbian heroine, indeed her disinterest in being remembered as a lesbian at all. In this way, Hammer is composing the queering of history, rather than lesbian history per se. She is recording the defiance of sexual categorization.

Hammer's acknowledgment of Eisenman's fluidity in the film and her resistance to circumscription within a prefigured category is particularly pointed because Eisenman is alive and capable of speaking for herself; Hammer can represent an argument over historical representation because Eisenman is quite literally arguing with her. But, in the segment featuring nineteenth-century artist Alice Austen, Hammer finds other ways to represent the long-deceased figure's resistance to recovery as a lesbian. Austen was an American photographer whose work has been celebrated by art historians despite the frequently controversial scenes she staged and photographed. One example of her work is a photograph of Austen and her girlfriends in men's clothing, hats, and artificial facial hair with a phallic umbrella cheekily placed between her knees (figure 3.1). These gender-bending photographs, along with her multidecade romantic relationship with Gertrude Tate, have compelled some historians to classify her as a lesbian, while other art historians have just as staunchly denied this classification. Therefore Austen's sexuality was already a source of contention between retroactivists who wanted to claim her for lesbian history and conservative art historians, such as the board of the Alice Austen House, who wanted to deny her sexuality.

Though Austen was no longer alive by the making of the film, Hammer's interviewees step in to resist her classification as a lesbian *for* her. Members of the Alice Austen House board defensively responded to Hammer's insistent questioning about Austen's sexuality with refusals to discuss it or to let researchers who intended to "out" Austen into their archives. While this response from the conservative historical society might be expected, resembling the exigency for the forms of retroactivism featured in earlier chapters, Hammer also includes less expected responses, further complicating the simplistic recovery of Austen into lesbian history. She interviews researcher Amy Khoudari with the same insistent questions she posed to Eisenman—questions about Austen's position as a lesbian

Fig. 3.1. Alice Austin and friends in drag, October 15, 1891. *Photo by Alice Austen; collection of Historic Richmond Town; courtesy of the Staten Island Historical Society*

foremother in the history of art—but Khoudari, a self-identifying lesbian, also refused to acquiesce on Austen's behalf. When Hammer directly asked Khoudari whether Austen was a lesbian, the researcher answered that Austen "wouldn't have considered herself one, because that wasn't defined the same as today. But I do think she thought of herself as a woman who loved women, who wasn't attracted to men." While Khoudari's voice argues with Hammer's appropriation, images of Austen's photographs are remediated in the film, their gender-bending and sexually ambiguous images conflicting with and supporting her words.

Through interviews coupled with remediated archival photographs, Hammer again showcases both the desire to claim historical figures into lesbian history *and* the need to resist this desire, revealing how the figure gainsays the present categories we overlay on the past. That is, while Austen could not speak for herself, Hammer recorded Khoudari's queering of Austen. On camera, Khoudari describes the ways that Austen herself defied then-present categories with her art and life, reading Austen's many photographs of her and her friends in costumes as an "opportunity to blur gender roles." Unlike many art historians, Khoudari reads Austen's photos of feminine dress (such as figure 3.2) as a comment on "society's regulations concerning sexualities" as much as the many cross-dressing photographs were (such as figure 3.1); the frilly dresses were as much a queer costume as the men's clothing. Viewers could then read the showcased photographs against Khoudari's descriptions.

One of the ways Austen resists primary classification in contemporary sexual categories is in her defiance of ethical and political standards of contemporary gay and lesbian historians. Alice Austen is revealed in *The Female Closet* to be a visionary artist, a gender iconoclast—and a staunch racist. Historians interviewed in the film describe Austen as a "powerfully destabilizing figure . . . because her rebellion is so deep and so intimate": a "rather butch" woman who owned and drove several cars when few women knew how to drive, made repairs on the cars herself, and lived with her longtime partner, Gertrude, for decades. But immediately following this

Fig. 3.2. "The Darned Club." *Photo by Alice Austen; collection of Historic Richmond Town; courtesy of the Staten Island Historical Society*

glowing recovery of an artist who bucked the gender conventions of her historical moment, Khoudari admits that "as much as I like Alice, she was a woman of her time. She was racist, an anti-Semite. I'm not going to make excuses because there is no excuse." Against Hammer-as-interviewer's pressure to glorify Austen for lesbian history, Khoudari insists that Alice Austen was "not a heroine": "people who knew her knew she was a nasty woman, an interesting bundle of contradictions." Austen's uglier side represents a challenge for historians who endeavor to populate the past with successful lesbians to legitimate a more equitable present.

Thus Hammer showcases rather than ignores the inexcusable flaws in her historical subjects, the attributes that progressive retroactivists would likely find distasteful. As Halberstam explains,

> As much as we have to excavate some histories that have been rendered invisible, we also bury others, and sometimes we do both at the same time. You could say that gay and lesbian scholars have also a hidden history, unsavory histories, and have a tendency to select from historical archives only the narratives that please (*Queer Art* 148).

Halberstam argues for a queer historiography that eschews the rescue of the "good gays" in anyone's determination and that is instead "resigned to the contradictory and complicit narratives that, in the past as in the present, connect sexuality to politics" (*Queer Art* 149). Nonnormative sexuality does not always map onto a rational, affirmative politics in which its figures emerge as heroic victims of a homophobic foe. Anticipating Halberstam's argument, Hammer attends to the worst attributes of her artist subjects—Alice Austen, Hannah Höch, and Nicole Eisenman—flaws she means not to glorify or even excuse because she cannot but rather to embrace their "contradictions" and "complicity" as well as their brilliance.

The rhetorical significance of this retroactivist strategy is in the interruption of viewers' affinity with Eisenman and Austen, their elevation of the artists as heroic foremothers. Viewers are left not with a canon of idealized lesbians but with the *slipperiness* of a canon, the evasion of Hammer's and perhaps their own attempts to claim identification with a successful artist. The gainsaying represented in the film models the queer historiographic process in which efforts to produce a glorified lineage of a lesbian past come into conflict with the flawed and agential humanity of its historical figures.

SHIFTING ALLEGIANCES AND RECONFIGURED MEMORY

Avoiding the challenges in composing lesbian history with appropriated figures in her 1996 film *Tender Fictions*, Hammer turns to her personal history of sexuality and her own archive of film footage, photographs, and memories. The fifty-eight-minute experimental documentary is ostensibly autobiographical, as it focuses on the filmmaker's life, but it is as much about the sexually identified communities she enters and breaks from as her life unfolds. Even as the film purports to be a history of Hammer's life as a lesbian, it calls into question whether it is possible to compose a history of sexuality as if sexual identity were enduring and unchanging through the course of a life. Because Hammer's sexuality was not constant, her history may not—or not always—be a lesbian history.

The particular multimodal rhetorical strategy enabling this complex historiography is *nonlinearity*. Jeff Rice defines multimodal nonlinearity as "various overlapping, nonsequential strands that one does not choose among but composes with simultaneously" (116). Rather than composing with one "strand of causality" or even multiple "individual alternative routes," nonlinearity "tells stories from multiple strands" at once (116). The strategy is particularly impactful in composing with memory—the recollection of the past in a present moment and circumstance—because there are always at least two stories in memory: the past and its present recollection.

As a result of this strategy of telling multiple stories at once, no single narrative of the past is figured as the Truth. As David Sheridan and coauthors contend, the inclusion of "multiple retellings of a single event" in films is a "multimodal rhetorical strategy" to make "audiences realize that meaning is dependent upon the way an event is depicted" (822). Instead of one version of "what happened," nonlinearity allows multiple tales of the past to be told at once, from different present moments. In Hammer's film, this strategy undermines a viewer's understanding of history as a series of "good gays" whose sexual identity endures through time, opening the historiographic field to multiple simultaneous alternatives.

Tender Fictions is an experimental, nonnarrative film without a plot, a pastiche of Hammer's personal archive of film footage of her own life that she assiduously recorded for more than thirty years. Hammer manipulates the footage with her signature technique of optical printing and overlays it with spoken quotations from philosophers and queer theorists. As the film unfolds, her collage of archival footage from her life suggests that her sexual identifications have shifted over time. Because she came out at thirty years of age sometime after the end of a heterosexual marriage, she found herself between communities, severed from her husband but not yet accepted by lesbian audiences. When Hammer entered a different community newly self-identified as a lesbian, her prior autobiographical footage conflicted with her emerging sense of self and new audience. In *Tender Fictions*, Hammer harnesses the strategy of nonlinearity to reconfigure the footage of her former heterosexual life so that it historicizes her current identification as a lesbian.

In one exemplary scene of multimodal nonlinearity, the middle-aged Hammer films herself slowly and carefully applying artificial facial hair, a bowling hat, and a tie (figure 3.3). While she dons her masculine attire, Hammer's disembodied voice describes an early memory from the perspective of herself as a child in third person:

> She looks in the mirror and examines her large broad face. Pitching her father's jaunty hat, something is missing. The charcoal on her cheek works well, giving her a five-o'clock shadow; the open blue collar of her dad's work shirt falls from her slight shoulders. The

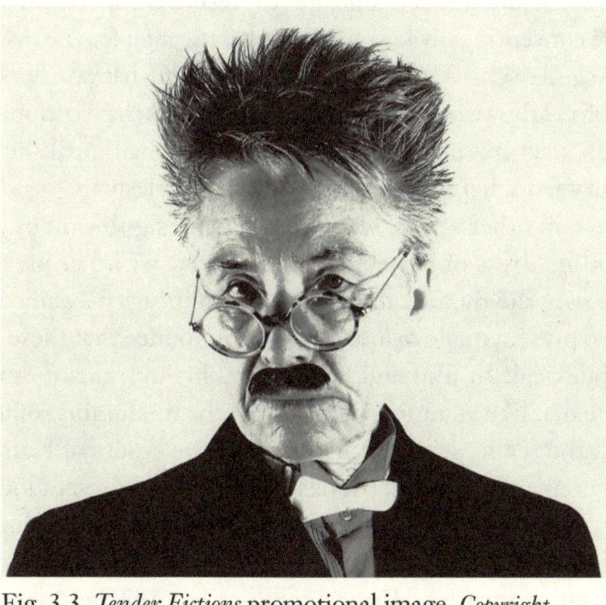

Fig. 3.3. *Tender Fictions* promotional image. *Copyright © Barbara Hammer*

> girl takes a comb, grabs her long brown hair in two handfuls, holds both below her chin and secures it with an elastic. She sprouts a new beard. I am 11 and cross-dressed for the first time. (*Tender Fictions*)

The visual footage of the middle-aged Hammer reveals that her hair is regularly cropped short now, no longer the brunette lengths of her youth described in her memory, and she takes on a masculine swagger. The dual modes—visual present and audio memory—allow her to inhabit two temporal moments simultaneously, evincing the nonlinear rhetorical strategy Rice describes. Further blurring temporality through nonlinearity, this footage is made to look archival even though it is clear from her age that this is the contemporary Hammer: it is slowed down like eight-millimeter film in a projector, faded and otherwise silent except for the narrated memory of childhood cross-dressing.

It is only after this scene that we discover that Hammer's memory of childhood cross-dressing was for a Halloween costume. Her memory of this costume, which had no apparent sexual significance at age eleven, takes on new meaning from her present position as a lesbian, a position of desire she maintains she never even considered until she was thirty years old. As Annamarie Jagose explains, "masculinity has persistently been the definitional ambit that enunciates the lesbian as spectacularly visible, lesbianism conventionally becoming legible through female masculinity's perceived clash of codes" (*Inconsequence* 3). Looking back on her childhood memory of a Halloween costume, Hammer invests that costume with new meaning, a meaning of sexual visibility it never had until she refigured the memory from her present identification as a lesbian.

Hammer, in other words, *makes* the memory significant by acting out the masculine dress of her childhood memory with her present, older body. She uses the rhetorical strategy of nonlinearity—audio memories and a video present made to look past—to announce that these memories are not indexical. In film and historiography, indexicality means that archival media, like an untouched photograph, maintains some material bond with the reality it traces. But because the events of Hammer's life are largely remembered as she looks back from her present location, the memories she represents are not indexical to the past. "I promise *not* to tell the truth," her voice speaks in the film, not "the whole truth," nor "nothing but the truth." Historiographically, the effect of the present invention and reconfiguration of memory is an undermining of any one version of the past. As Rice explains, "it is up to the reader to engage with these strands, reading them together or separately, to see them in conversation with one another or not, and to forge a variety of connections the author intended or didn't intend to occur" (119).[8]

There is no Truth to be told of Hammer's past: even the memories she holds at one point elude her later, change on her, take on new meaning as her life unfolds. When Hammer repeats a sound clip at different points in the film, juxtaposed with different archival images from her life, she prompts the viewer to question the authenticity of previous iterations and to find that each juxtaposition might be equally true. For instance, periodically throughout the film, a quotation is repeated by a low, disembodied voice, out of sync with any moving images: "Autobiography is not a timeless process but is embedded in ongoing history in the search for the identity of the individual and the communities in which she lives." This repeated quotation from French philosopher Georges Gusdorf situates Hammer's personal story and archive in a broader, ongoing—that is, changing and adaptive—lesbian history and a plurality of shifting communities.

To express this shifting, unreliable record of change multimodally, Hammer repeats the exact phrases she used to narrate her life with her husband when she later narrates her new life with Florrie, her current domestic partner. In recalling the motorcycle tour of Europe she took with her husband, Hammer narrates that "the smell of diesel fuel brings back the memory of early mornings. We drove through Syria, Turkey, Iraq, until he fell from the machine, weak from the jaundice he picked up from the aluminum poles of the tent he bought second-hand in Florence." This audio memory is spoken over archival footage filmed from the back of the motorcycle, while she is clinging to the back of her then-husband. She claims at this point that the present waft of diesel reminds her of those times; yet later in the film, spoken over several photographs of her and Florrie standing next to motorcycles and riding in Pride parades, she speaks this: "the smell of diesel fuel brings back early memories of the tent I bought second hand in Italy." The smell has changed the memory it recalls: who bought the tent and was she now alone then? Must she change those memories with her husband to historicize her present identity as a lesbian? Or are the memories already inaccessible, able only to be constructed from her present perspective? The use of multimodal nonlinearity to disrupt any certainty about the past makes each past equally possible.

Hammer, however, seeks some redress to this uncertainty and instability. Late in the film, she returns to another childhood memory, evincing more nonlinear chronology, and articulates the memory as a parable for how she might continue to compose history when memory fails. Against the image of the lights and shadows of a tree in a suburban yard, her voice narrates:

> In the back yard, there was an old nectarine tree the children liked to play beneath. We would bury the toys and dig them up again in the spring. It was a memory game and *if one couldn't find a toy, the other one might, so history could be told and retold.* Today when I eat an overripe nectarine in the heat of summer, I remember a toy I never found.

The present cues of memory summon a past that cannot be found in totality; only its loss can be located, a "toy I never found." But this is Hammer's attempt at redress: histories are to be told collectively, with others, so that when memory fails, when the past cannot be found, another might find it and so "history can be told and retold."

These second-hand histories of her life are found by Hammer when she solicits and records her attempts to find herself through other people, by taping her calls to her old friends and lovers and asking them to tell her their favorite "lesbian memories" of her and their worst. These voices are witnesses and *participants* in her historiography, making it collective because as she has shown, she cannot write history alone. A different woman's voice answers the phone call each time, sometimes expressing admiration, sometimes a trivial memory, but more often expressing an emotional or critical response to Hammer: "I remember a story going around about you when you broke up with Terry Sendgraft. Someone asked you why you broke up with her and you said it was because she got more phone calls than you." The next woman (perhaps Terry, but it is unclear) speaks this: "I thought you were treating me like I was a piece of furniture, a chair you could sit on. You were treating me like an object. It was hardest for me when you were wrapped up in trying to get the world to give you what you want." These "archival records" seem the most authentic for Hammer in her search for her past lived among and against others: the confessions of lost loves, the gossip overheard, the "toys" found by someone else so "history can be told and retold."

"IMAGING" TABOOS AND EXPOSING EXCLUSION

Hammer's willingness to expose herself in her films is not limited to her own flaws, body, and secrets. The third historiographic innovation I identify is the deliberate and sustained depiction of taboos in images, without apology, critique, or attempts to conform to social mores. Through this tactic, the margins of the margins are made central. In this section, I focus on Barbara Hammer's 1992 film, *Nitrate Kisses*, a sixty-seven-minute experimental documentary. Announcing itself as a distinctly historiographic film, *Nitrate Kisses* opens with a quotation from Adrienne Rich:

> Whatever is unnamed, undepicted in images, whatever is omitted from biography, censored in collections of letters, whatever is misnamed as something else, made difficult-to-come-by, whatever is buried in the memory by the collapse of meaning under an inadequate or lying language—this will become, not merely unspoken, but unspeakable.

From this opening quotation from Rich, we learn that the film will be about the present dangers of allowing the past to become or remain "unspeakable," proscribed. *Nitrate Kisses* is an attempt to redress these dangers by deliberately showcasing the taboo images and stories that are silenced even *within* lesbian communities and history. Hammer stages and films these taboo images, and displays them in front of a backdrop of oral history interviews with lesbians who have faced discrimination within their own communities.

The film utilizes the multimodal rhetorical strategy of "imaging" to showcase taboos. Drawing on neuroscience and cognitive psychology, Joddy Murray emphasizes the fundamental role of the image in symbol use, arguing that "our brains function through image" in powerful ways:

> Image is not only a basic unit of thought in the brain—the progenitor of language and a component of reason—but image also *shapes* the brain, constructs pathways and nodes which make up such potentialities as personality, health, and acumen. In other words, there are structural and functional elements in the brain that point to the centrality of image to thought—displacing alphacentric language. (6, his emphasis)

Images, he suggests, do far more than approximate an external reality; they can fashion our bodily experience and affective responses to the world.

I suggest that images of taboos—ineffable bodies, acts, and qualities—can bypass language and affect viewers more viscerally. This section addresses the strategic use of filmed images to compose history that shocks viewers, even and especially viewers who identify as lesbians. Because the imaging occurs in a film, it is a multimodal composition with duration and, in *Nitrate Kisses*, the temporality of film forces the viewer to linger on unsettling historical images, increasing the viewer's exposure to taboos. The rhetorical effect is to encourage the viewer to redress the exclusions that the sustained attention of the film gradually makes appear unnecessary.

Soon after the opening quotation from Adrienne Rich on the dangers of historical suppression, *Nitrate Kisses* showcases two nude, elderly, white women engaged in explicit sexual acts, shot with an intimate camera moving deftly around the couple (figure 3.4). The images are certainly taboo, depicting pornographic images of women far older than the youthful prime celebrated by the industry. Voyeuristically, Hammer films the couple in black-and-white through the shifting shadows of leaves of plants, cutting to footage of ruined buildings to suggest that, like these ruins, aged lesbian bodies are abandoned.

These taboo images are affective but they also have meaning, inflected by the unsynced soundtrack. While the images play on the screen, a group of elderly women's voices describe their memories growing up gay. The unnamed voices share memories of life in New York's Christopher Street bars in the forties and fifties; memories of close gay male friends lost to AIDS; memories of working in factories during World War II; memories of first sexual experiences; memories of finding space to be together in public. A few women's memories particularly articulate Hammer's motivations for displaying taboo images. One woman's voice shares an experience in Prospect Park when she and her lover were pelted with rocks by neighborhood boys before a disembodied scholarly voice cautions against the narrowness of the dichotomous categories "gay" and "straight," and encourages "orders of analysis more complex than binary oppositions." A second woman's memory then complicates the homophobic, straight-opposing-gay conclusions of the first woman's memory in the park. This woman sadly admits that "there is a lot of

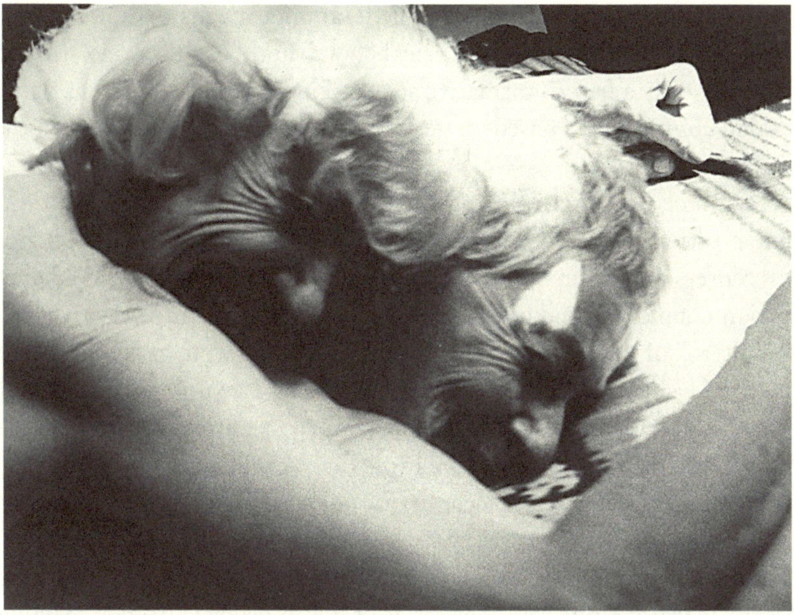

Fig. 3.4. Still from *Nitrate Kisses. Copyright © Barbara Hammer*

ageism in the lesbian community. I felt, and feel, invisible. Invisible." A third woman shares a similar sense of being left behind by a lesbian community as times, fashions, and gender expectations changed: "Things began to change, I was looked down upon by other lesbians [because of my masculine appearance]. I felt like an outcast. Lesbians were beginning to look like women. Couples looked feminine. I was like . . . what? I don't know what's going on here."

These collected, disembodied aural fragments, played over the aged bodies of an intimate lesbian couple, suggest that Hammer's taboo images expose the fractures within lesbian communities. Hammer supports this intention with a quotation from Foucault, boldly printed in white on a black screen:

> If repression has indeed been the fundamental link between power, knowledge, and sexuality since the classical age, it stands to reason that we will not be able to free ourselves from it except at a considerable cost: nothing less than a transgression of laws, a lifting of prohibitions, an interruption of speech, a reinstating of pleasure within reality, and a whole new economy in the mechanisms of power will be required.

By making taboos shockingly visible, Hammer means to "interrupt the speech," to transgress the historical "laws" and "prohibitions" that inform not only a heteronormative society but also the repressions within lesbian communities based on gender performance, age, race, and other differences.

Hammer reinforces this point throughout the film with additional juxtapositions of taboo images set against verbalized examples of historical repression within oppressed groups. She films a tattooed and pierced lesbian couple in bondage and backs images of their intimacy with the soundtrack of the disembodied voice of a German woman describing the plight of lesbians during the Nazi occupation. The unidentified woman describes the hierarchy within the woman's concentration camp Ravensbrück: "the other women, the heterosexuals, the Jewish women, and the women in the concentration camps for political reasons, they could raise up their voices . . . their social statuses were better" than the "prostitutes, criminals, and asocials"—the latter a category that included lesbians. After the war, no one told the stories of these "asocial" women, who had no one to "listen to their stories" even though some of them had survived to tell them. The unnamed speaker contends that these survivors had to claim they were "nowhere" between the years of the war, in another country, to hide the stigma of being imprisoned for sexual deviance. And later, even if someone asked, the narrator explains, they no longer "had words for it. For so many years, nobody asked, and then, when someone did, they have [*sic*] no answer anymore. The silence inside them is so deep, so it is very hard to find out what happened in this time." With taboo images overlaying tales of silence, Hammer highlights exclusionary practices within communities defined by oppression.

By playing the story of these silenced—and then silent—historical women behind the images of a contemporary, heavily tattooed and pierced BDSM couple and intercut footage of abandoned concentration camps in ruins, Hammer prompts viewers to examine their own perpetuation of exclusions, both in present communities and in historical recovery. BDSM has had a vexed position within feminist history for its eroticization of domination, but Hammer suggests that any exclusion based on sexuality from within the lesbian community perpetuates exclusions suffered *by* the community. She eschews narrative structure, constructing the entire film solely with juxtapositions of incongruent, taboo images and an unsynced soundtrack of interviews with unidentified voices. Thus, in both form and content, Hammer attempts to undo the "laws" and "prohibitions," undermining the notion of taboo by making boldly controversial images visible, sustained, and unavoidable.

MANIPULATING AND INVENTING THE QUEER ARCHIVE

Traditional historiography depends on the credibility of the archive, which is enhanced when the archival material remains in its unadulterated, original form and indicates an accurate description of events it purports to describe. But this approach to the archive often has less to offer queer historians, who seek to unearth a past of "intimacy, sexuality, love, and activism" that is historically elided by official archives and challenging to preserve anyway (Cvetkovich, "In the Archive" 110). The filmic historiographers investigated in this section employ multimodal rhetorical strategies to disrupt the dependence of retroactivism on unadulterated, original archival materials—by purposefully manipulating and even *inventing* archival materials.

The first film discussed in this section is Hammer's *History Lessons* (2000), a sixty-five-minute experimental documentary that employs the strategy of appropriation to manipulate materials from "straight" archives (archives that represent normative intimacy, couples, families). Rice defines "appropriation" as a multimodal rhetorical strategy through which existing media are strategically employed in new compilations. These new compilations become "mash-ups" or "cutups," a genre in which a composer appropriates existing "language, text, image, and ideas in order to fashion critiques of media and ideology" (Rice 57). In *History Lessons* Hammer appropriates straight archival media, mashing them together and dubbing new voices onto archival video to construct a lesbian world that never existed—but could have.

The second film is Dunye's 1996 *The Watermelon Woman*, which appropriates the genre of the archive. Inventing an archive from scratch, Dunye fabricates photographs to tell the historiographic story of the search for an African American lesbian who never existed, but like Hammer's manipulated archival world, *could* have. Dunye's films offer a much-needed racial consciousness to historiographic retroactivism that Hammer's films are largely missing.

In each case, the appropriations are "honest." The historiographic strategy of fictitious archives reveals its deception to viewers through the obviousness of the archive's overt manipulation. Yet even after the viewer has been assured the archive is invented or modified, the use of multimodal technologies—and the power of the authentic-looking photographic image—can make the viewer disbelieve the deception and seek to find some truth in it anyway. It is in this simultaneous deception and belief that the multimodal rhetorical strategy of appropriation finds its efficacy in historiography. Viewers' sense of historical accuracy is undermined, but they are prompted to find some other kind of truth in the composition nonetheless.

Manipulating History Lessons

Hammer's *History Lessons* is composed of manipulated and selectively intercut film clips and still photographs from straight archives, modified and rearranged to reveal lesbian history in unexpected places. In an interview about the film, Hammer explains that she took images "made by men" and "reconfigured them, edited them, montaged them, [and] put them together in a new way to show lesbian power. A representation of a world that never existed before" (Hammer, "Special Feature").

Hammer can be understood as an extreme example of what Morris calls an "archival queer": one who enters "the history housed in straight archives and circulated in straight collections"; "understands the archive's promise as an inventional wellspring"; and, with "ingenuity, tenacity, and voice," troubles "sexual normalcy and its discriminations" ("Archival Queers" 148). Hammer inventively troubles sexual normalcy in the straight archive by, quite obviously, *modifying* gender and sexually normative cultural texts—filmed speeches, educational videos from the 1950s, military recruitment videos, vintage 1920s pornography—so that, with the right editing, these normalizing artifacts become evidence of lesbian history. She does so to make lesbian history "visible" in the heterosexual- and male-constructed film narratives, because she assumes these narratives obscure the existence of a lesbian past that she is sure was there, a lesbian past that could be there if not for the culturally enforced erasure of nonnormative sexuality.[9]

In one memorable example, Hammer opens *History Lessons* with an archival film clip of Eleanor Roosevelt preparing to address a women's conference in the 1920s. An unnamed woman introduces Roosevelt to the audience of women, asserting that "no one knows our country better than Eleanor Roosevelt, no one knows [dubbed: *lesbians*] better than her." While the visual footage of the conference is authentic, Hammer manipulates the sound to replace the original speaker's "women" with an obviously dubbed "lesbians." After Roosevelt addresses the assembly of women, another speaker is dubbed to declare that "dykes are people too" and then continues in her original voice, arguing that "the constitution is the supreme law of the land. Therefore these rights have been guaranteed to us. We have the right [dubbed: *to be gay and make love to whom we want*]." In this manipulated clip, Hammer queers the straight archive by making lesbian history where it wasn't. But, at the same time, her manipulation of Eleanor Roosevelt isn't entirely untrue. As I noted above, several historians have speculated about the nature of the First Lady's romantic affection for journalist Lorena Hickok.[10] In *History Lessons*, Hammer invented an archive to retroactively provide evidence for a same-sex relationship that is the source of ongoing speculation.

At the same time, however, Hammer undermines the evidence she invents by making clear that her manipulations of the archive are appropriations. Her dubbed-over lines are spoken in a falsetto voice that no viewer would mistake for the speaker's original voice. According to Rice, multimodal appropriation is a way to restructure language and thought because strategic appropriations of dominant texts are "both ideological (resistance to dominant thinking) and rhetorical (generating new thought)" (62). Through appropriation, Hammer is resisting the ideological primacy of the straight archive and generating the rhetorical possibility of a lesbian past. Yet Hammer's "appropriation" is honest. Viewers know immediately that she is modifying the archive because her technique is intentionally crude and obvious. It is a call to action for viewers to boldly enter straight archives and queer things up: a rhetorical strategy to desanctify the archive, reduce its hallowed status as the foundation of (hetero)history and instead use the archive's material to construct a world that "could have been."

The remainder of the film is a pastiche of manipulated found footage of 1950s educational videos, the 1940s Women's Army Corps, female boxers, and many other black-and-white clips from the archive, which do not contain representations of "proved" lesbians but are "lesbianized" through their arrangement and dubbed-over sound. For instance, Hammer takes a 1950s educational video about a group of young women learning about the new invention of parking meters and strategically intercuts it with vintage 1920s pornography, made "lesbian" by editing to remove the men. The story told by these mashed-up archival clips becomes the tale of a group of young women who get ticketed for failing to put another nickel in the meter because they are "distracted" upstairs (what they are distracted by is implied by the vintage pornographic clips).[11]

Similar archival mash-ups are constructed out of clips of the Women's Army Corps, clips of female athletes boxing and exercising, and other footage from the archive.[12] These clips are "cut up" from their contexts and rearranged in new compositions to tell stories different from those the original, intact footage intended. In so doing, Hammer begins to change the meaning of the straight archive she samples from. Despite occasional dark images, such as a clip from a nineteenth-century snuff film,[13] *History Lessons* is a comedy, a whimsical romp into straight archives where queerness could have been. Once inside the archive, Hammer selects and edits film clips into a new arrangement to showcase, she asserts, "lesbian power," using dubbing and mash-up to make historical figures speak as lesbians regardless of their self-identification. These historical figures become participants in the composition of lesbian history, appropriated by Hammer to populate the past.

Honest Deceptions in The Watermelon Woman*: Inventing the Archive*

More audaciously than Hammer's manipulation of straight archives, Dunye actually *invents* an archive from scratch to recover a fictional African American lesbian. Her 1996 film *The Watermelon Woman* is a "dunyementary," a "hybrid of narrative, documentary, comedy, and autobiography" (Juhasz 291). The ninety-minute film is less a history itself than a film about historiographic excavation, focusing on the impact of race and class in veiling potentially queer historical figures. The film documents the process of a fictional search for queer history through the "video diaries" of the lead character, footage of her investigation, and an archive of black-and-white photos and films.

Dunye plays herself in the film: "Cheryl," a twenty-five-year-old black lesbian who works in a video store, videotapes weddings for extra cash, and wants to become a filmmaker. Dissatisfied with her perennially single life and her nonexistent film career, Cheryl is simply "waiting" for a film concept to come, knowing it "has to be about black women because our stories aren't told." While watching a (fake) film from the 1930s, "Plantation Memories," she becomes fascinated with the beautiful "mammy" character and is shocked to see the woman credited only as "The Watermelon Woman" at the end of the film. Finally inspired, Cheryl sets out to make a documentary of the mystery woman's life, eventually discovering that she is "Fae Richards," a 1930s-era, African American actress who "could have existed" but never actually did, except in the context of Dunye's film (Juhasz 291).

While Hammer's use of appropriation depends on modifying and mashing up existing straight archives, Dunye's use of appropriation is even more radical. By making her own archive to historicize the invented Fae Richards, she appropriates the genre of the archive—capitalizing on its authority to set the "conditions of possibility which shaped what could be written" (Stoler 91). Dunye appropriates the archive's authorization of the stories that can be told in order to make Richards's story possible. But, because her archive is fictional, she at the same time undermines the sanctity of the archive as the foundational source for history. In other words, Dunye appropriates the authority of the archive to produce Fae Richards, while at the same time calling archives into question for their erasure of anyone like Richards. In this tension, her historiographic retroactivism emerges.

Like Hammer's appropriations, Dunye's deceptions are honest: the final credits reveal the glamorous archival photos and film clips from the 1930s featured in *The Watermelon Woman* actually star a contemporary young actress shot by a contemporary photographer. When the credits finish rolling, Dunye prints a quotation from herself on screen: "Sometimes you have to create your own history. The Watermelon Woman is fiction." Yet at the same time as viewers are made aware that Richards wasn't real, the photographs and film clips are so vividly realistic in the film, so skillfully aged and styled to look authentically archival that the viewer can forget, or even refuse to believe, that they are constructed. As Robert Reid-Pharr writes,

> the film does its work too well. Dunye uncovers the way an essentially materialist conception of history has become so deeply ingrained in our discourses of identity that, even when audiences are told explicitly that the object they are being offered is fake, they will insist on the object's authenticity if it is offered alongside a formulaic allegiance to the notion of a material reality behind the ephemeral image. (131–32)

The illusion of authenticity sits in tension with the film's outright honesty about its invention of the archive.

The archive isn't real but it *feels* real, which opens up the possibility for a different kind of knowing. Saidiya Hartman calls this kind of knowing a "critical fabulation" that is past-conditional, that could have been if only racial and sexual bias hadn't rendered figures like Richards invisible in the historical record (11). This kind of knowing, in other words, is "subjunctive"—it is unreal, a fantasy, a wishfulness for what could have been but wasn't. The film historizes loss, performing the methods of history to expose what and whom is made "absent, entangled, and unavailable by its methods" (Hartman 11). In documenting Cheryl's excavation of Richards, Dunye films historiographic methods to *create* a fantasy history that would have been left absent, entangled, and unavailable by those very methods—had she not overstepped them by inventing the archive in the first place.

This film is about how very difficult it is to find women like Richards who were marginalized in their own moment and erased from ours because of her race, gender, and sexuality. Dunye films "Cheryl" following a chain of mostly dead-end research: she interviews strangers in the street, her mother who "saw all the movies in the 30s" and "saved everything," the male owner of "Race Films" who knows nothing of black women, and the local library, whose librarian can only tell her to check the "film," "women," or "black" sections. While none of these leads take her to the Watermelon Woman, Cheryl manages to locate her mother's old friend Shirley, who remembers visiting lesbian clubs where the Watermelon Woman once sang. Shirley knows the woman's "real" name, Fae Richards, and tells Cheryl that Richards had a relationship with her white female director, Martha Page. By filming her chain of mostly dead-end research and the fruits of Shirley's gossip, Dunye is "documenting the archive itself," in Cvetkovich's terms: the queer archive, which circulates in gaps in libraries and rumors among friends of friends ("In the Archives" 114). Yet Dunye takes her documentation of the archive a step further, since the archive and the historical figure she seeks in it are both fabrications from the start.

In performing and filming this artificial search, Dunye intimates that what is found in the search for queer history is always in some sense a fiction of the historian's present, a retroactivist project she performs—at least in part—for herself. This is clear in Cheryl's response to a letter sent to her by Fae Richards's former longtime love, June, a black woman who warns Cheryl not to focus on Richards's relationship with Martha Page, since doing so would obscure a wholly African American history of Richards that could stand as a tradition for future black lesbian film artists. Cheryl ultimately takes control of Richards's history, deciding that her recovery of Richards is for *her*. She speaks into her video diary a message for June: "I know she meant the world to you, but she meant the world to me too. And our worlds are different. What she means to me, a twenty-five-year-old black woman, it means something else: hope, inspiration, possibility, history." She decides, with this statement, that she must find her own meaning, and *use*, from the history she composes, even if her figures object to her representation of them, because the history she composes is as much about her as it is about her subjects. The fictionality of her subject and archive, the fact that Fae Richards never existed, reinforces the implication that queer historiography is about what the search and the subjects mean for the present.

Dunye's film is taking and granting a license to invent the histories concealed by racial, gender, and sexual biases in the historical record. She and Zoe Leonard, the photographer of Richards's fake archive, made the authentic-looking images of "Richards" into a book, published separately from the film. The book, *The Fae Richards Photo Archive, 1993–1996*, showcases the staged documentation of the fictional 1930s actress and itself becomes a part of the evolving queer archive. Leonard's book contains seventy-eight black-and-white seemingly authentic photographs, four-color photographs, and a handwritten notebook, with photos often captioned with hand-scrawled phrases like "me and the girls at the Hotspot." The book and its filmic inspiration suggests that contemporary queer historiography is about *documenting the search*, rather than finding the figure sought, and sometimes, the search documented is the search for the present queer self—though neither figure can be securely fixed or located, as both Hammer (*Tender Fictions*) and Dunye suggest. Figures past and present can, however, be *invented* through multimodal appropriation of the genre of the archive.

PERFORMING CAMP HISTORIOGRAPHY

This final section examines a film that frames *performance* as historiographic material. Like the anecdotes employed by the Daughters of Bilitis and the short-lived zines preserved by LHA, performance is a kind of ephemeral evidence endemic to the queer archive. But performance is strategically more elusive than other forms of ephemera, "meant to be interacted with by those within its epistemological sphere—while evaporating at the touch of those who would eliminate queer possibility" (Muñoz, "Ephemera" 6). And yet, though performance is ephemeral, Muñoz maintains that "performances of lived experience" sustain "experiential politics and urgencies long after these structures of feeling have been lived"; the effects of performance can linger as a "residue" in the public sphere with "powerful worldmaking capabilities ("Ephemera" 10–11). Captured to some degree by film, this residue can exceed the location and moment of the original performance.

Not Just Passing Through (1994) is a sixty-minute documentary produced by Jean Carlomusto, Dolores Perez, Catherine Gund Saalfield, and Polly Thistlewaite (an LHA archivette). Much of the film serves as an "advertisement to the Lesbian Herstory Archives" (Freydberg 1211), beginning with the parade inaugurating LHA's new home in Brooklyn in June 1993 before moving through interview- and archival-based accounts of Mabel Hampton (an elderly black member of the LHA collective), Marge McDonald (a white lesbian whose personal records were rescued by LHA from her ashamed family), and an Asian-American lesbian collective. Throughout the film, women from a variety of cultural and racial backgrounds emphasize how history has actively omitted "women loving women."

Of interest here is the concluding segment of the film, which features the Five Lesbian Brothers, a troupe of playwrights and performers named Moe Angelos, Babs Davy, Dominique Dibbell, Peg Healey, and Lisa Kron. Founded in 1989, the group composed a number of feminist lesbian-themed plays, often performing them at the WOW Café Theatre in New York City (a collectively run women's, lesbian, and transgender theater space). In *Not Just Passing Through*, a performance is captured and cut between interviews with the members of the Five Lesbian Brothers, who explain their motivations and rhetorical choices in the writing of the script and the direction of the acting.

The performance featured is *Brave Smiles . . . Another Lesbian Tragedy*, a historiographic two-act play in which the Brothers repurpose "archival materials," collecting and splicing iconic scenes from pulp fiction and sensationalist films. Healey explains that they

> watched, read, listened to, explored, and absorbed every possible lesbian icon we could get our hands on and shamelessly used them for our purposes. If the story of the lesbian is that she was always doomed to suffer an unhappy life and then die a tragic death, then we really wanted to pile it on. (Five Lesbian Brothers 44)

The Brothers' archive of references for the play exceeded fifteen films and books from between 1928 and 1977 that "doomed" the lesbian to that "unhappy life" and "tragic death," including

- *The Well of Loneliness* (1928 novel by Radclyffe Hall)
- *Morocco* (1930 film starring Marlene Dietrich)
- *Maedchen in Uniform* (1931 German film)
- *The Price of Salt* (1952 novel by Patricia Highsmith)
- *Johnny Guitar* (1954 film starring Joan Crawford)
- *Beebo Brinker* (1957–62 pulp fiction series by Ann Bannon)
- *I Want to Live* (1958 film starring Susan Hayward)
- *The Children's Hour* (1961 film starring Audrey Hepburn and Shirley MacLaine)
- *Walk on the Wild Side* (1962 film starring Jane Fonda and Barbara Stanwyck)
- *The Killing of Sister George* (1968 film starring Beryl Reid)
- *Julia* (1977 film starring Jane Fonda)

These sources were not arbitrarily chosen but selected for their ambivalent resonance in the lives of women with same-sex desire who had grown up in the twentieth century without other representations of lesbians. In an interview in *Not Just Passing Through*, Healey explains her own experience growing up with the pulps and films in this archive:

> I was constantly looking for lesbian images. . . . All the images that I found were very depressing and sad, and I really bought into that: lesbians are sad people, they end up lonely, they never have sex, they never have one lifetime partner. They die. . . . It seems like in the popular image to get acceptance was to have some grave disease, to die, to become noble through some kind of suffering.

Suggesting the enduring resonance of these images, Lisa Kron jokes later in this documentary that the Brothers were not able to rehearse regularly because they all had therapy on different nights.

Brave Smiles exaggerates the archive's tragic plotlines until they become humorous. The play begins in a European girl's school, where a militant German headmistress, a young, bewitching female teacher, and five female students engage in secret rendezvous and innuendos. Time passes and the students soon disperse across the continent, partaking in stereotypical lesbian activities like tennis, passing as men in the military, and prison. But methodically throughout the play, after each momentary flash of lesbian love, characters meet absurdly wretched ends, ranging from alcoholism and suicide to loneliness and addiction to a malignant brain tumor. After each tragedy, a bead is added to a "Necklace of Tears," which is passed between the survivors until, by the end of the play, the necklace becomes a noose.

Individually, the plots and images are painful and hopeless, but the Brothers' strategy to deplete their negative affect was to humorously overdramatize them and splice them together into a single performance. As Babs Davy notes in *Not Just Passing Through*, "If you add it all up together, it does become a farce." Through these interviews with the Brothers, the film reveals a retroactivist purpose of exaggerated performance. Kron explains in her filmed interview that "we're interested not just in parodying [the archive of films and books]; we're interested in how our lives are *shaped* by them." By splicing together and exaggerating many melancholic cultural images of lesbians, and then explaining their intentions in interviews, the performers deplete some of the more subtle power the images wielded individually. At the same time, they honor the images' impact on, as they say, the "lesbian psyche," by drawing these images together in one place—knowing they will be recognizable to their primarily lesbian audience. As Linda Hutcheon explains, humorous exaggeration both "legitimates and subverts that which it parodies" (101). Dominique Dibbell echoes Hutcheon in her filmed interview: "I love—LOVE—*The Well of Loneliness*. . . . We don't have to do that much to parody it; it's already funny when we play it straight in this context."

The performance of lesbian history through dramatic exaggeration of meaningful cultural images operates through what I call a *camp historiography*. To camp is a historiographic act already because, as Mark Booth maintains, "camp takes styles from the past and uses them to sidestep the onward march of history" (144). Like the Five Lesbian Brothers' description of their relationship to the pulps and films, camp's use of the past has a complex relationship with nostalgia. As Pamela Robertson argues, "camp redefines and historicizes" cultural artifacts like the films and pulps, "not only nostalgically but with a critical recognition of the temptation to nostalgia, rendering both the object and the nostalgia outmoded through an ironic, laughing distanciation" (267). A camp historiography, in other words, *performs* cultural artifacts with all the feeling of nostalgia but simultaneously drains some of the painful affect associated with the cultural artifacts through laughter.

Camp historiographic performance has the potential to alter viewers' relationship with melancholy narratives: to help them laugh, strategically, with—and at—nostalgia. The camp impulse can be read as a move to acknowledge and make visible, rather than deny or hide, painful or ugly pasts. As Love contends, the "emphasis on damage" in queer culture "exists in a state of tension with a related and contrary tendency—the need to resist damage and to affirm queer existence" (3). The exaggerated performance of tragic plots makes them self-conscious and conspicuous, and when the exaggeration is amplified through many hyperbolic scenes, the pain attached to the sources becomes available for both laughter and critique. As Angelos maintains, *Brave Smiles* "asks the audience why they are laughing and are they sure they are not crying" (Five Lesbian Brothers 44).

Here camp historiography becomes both rhetorical and potentially political. Performance scholar Peggy Phelan explains that *Brave Smiles* demonstrates how sourcing from melancholy artifacts "can generate both great comedy and an alternative political and performance tradition. . . . The repetitive accumulation of these lesbian tragedies inspires the audience to crave some other outcome, not only in the play but in life too" (xiv, xvii). This is what Muñoz means when he says that performance is the kind of ephemera that leaves a residue with "powerful world-making possibilities" ("Ephemera" 11).

CONCLUSION

Amid the emergence of New Queer Cinema, queer activism, and queer theory, the 1990s witnessed a number of films dedicated to extending and complicating the project of retroactivism. Filmmakers like Barbara Hammer, Cheryl Dunye, Jean Carlomusto, Dolores Perez, Catherine Gund Saalfield, Polly Thistlewaite, Su Friedrich, and Joan E. Biren set out to compose lesbian history with critical awareness of how intracommunity exclusions, the fluidity of sexuality, the enduring trauma of beloved cultural artifacts, and other complications challenged any endeavor to shape an enduring lineage of lesbian heroines. This chapter identifies five multimodal strategies in this work: (*1*) gainsaying, which captures the dialogic altercation between a historian and her subject's resistance to fixed and contemporary sexual identity categories; (*2*) nonlinearity, a strategy that captures the complexity of composing history with memory and acknowledges that sexuality can shift over the course of a lifetime; (*3*) the affective impact of taboo images, which has the potential to uncover exclusions within lesbian communities; (*4*) the manipulation and outright invention of archival evidence as a multimodal strategy for finding lesbian history where it could have been and for desanctifying the straight archive as the foundation of history; and (*5*) camp historiography, the performative exaggeration of iconic cultural artifacts as a strategy to both honor and critique nostalgia through laughter. These five rhetorical strategies demonstrate a kind of *historiographic* retroactivism: a queer approach that puts pressure on the logic of simplistic recovery and calls transhistoricist accounts of sexual identity into question.

The next and final chapter takes up some of the questions evoked by the challenges to identity and history, and the use of different technologies of historical production suggested in this chapter. The appropriation and remediation of archives and archival materials by filmmakers like Hammer, Dunye, and Carlomusto and her colleagues raise questions about how the compositions by earlier generations of retroactivists are framed and reframed by future generations of retroactivists in response to new exigencies and political objectives. What kind of legacy is created as retroactivists reference and remediate the fruits of prior generations? The affordance of film in remediating archival media also raises questions about the role of different technologies of historical production in enabling and constraining particular strategies, identities, and relations to the past itself. As the next chapter inquires, what happens when retroactivism goes digital?

4. "A HISTORY OF DISCONTINUITIES"

ON THE PAST AND FUTURE OF RETROACTIVISM

> If we look to the margins, to the ruptures and breaks, we will be able to piece together a history of women speaking to each other. Nevertheless, lesbian history will remain a history of discontinuities.
>
> —Martha Vicinus, "They Wonder to Which Sex I Belong"

> Machines, of course, do not make history by themselves. But some kinds of machines help make different kinds of histories and different kinds of people than others.
>
> —Susan J. Douglas, *Listening In*

Histories and archives of "lesbianism" have indeed been composed by communities who sought to create both change and stasis in their present worlds. Del Martin and Phyllis Lyon curated brief, encapsulated experiences of Daughters of Bilitis (DOB) women loving and living with women, and then archived the anecdotes in *Lesbian/Woman* in middle-class categories such as "motherhood" and "monogamous love." Apparent in the evidence of readers' letters was a palpable sense of collective identity shaped by the evolving archive of past experiences, based in conventions of femininity, motherhood, monogamy, and distinction from the queer bar scene. But pasts like those composed by the DOB can only be partial, as exemplified by readers' letters detailing feelings of despair and exclusion. Masculine gender identity and butch-femme relationship models were not accidentally absent from the DOB's archives of experience but actively excluded. Any history of lesbianism will be a "history of discontinuities"—replete with "ruptures and breaks" and painful absences (Vicinus 433).

Yet as Vicinus suggests, these fissures are precisely where we should look to suture a desultory "history of women speaking to each other" (433).

For like the history of lesbianism, the legacy of retroactivism is itself dis/continuous. While the Lesbian Herstory Archives (LHA) preserves and even features the DOB within its vast and eclectic collections, I am uncertain whether the more conservative DOB would have archived LHA. In contrast to the DOB's written composition of clustered, middle-class anecdotes, LHA's primary medium for composing the past was material archivization: the collection and arrangement of artifacts and records. LHA sought to challenge bias and exclusion in traditional archives and libraries by classifying differently: through radically inclusive yet separatist procedures for selecting and arranging archival materials. Through strategies of classifying material artifacts, LHA arranged multiplicitous and contradictory materials representing diverse identities (including sex-positive feminists, working-class butches, bisexual women, transwomen, and transmen) and blurred the boundaries between archival categories to draw associations across the diversity.

Yet, despite the more eclectic elements of LHA collections in comparison with the DOB, the pasts each collective composed are discontinuously *linked* in a legacy of retroactivism, for as Vicinus argues, there are "connections embedded in differences and contradictions" in lesbian historiography (433). LHA and the DOB are linked through their efforts to compose the past in response to then-present exigencies—the ascription of pathology and criminality to women with same-sex desire, the accompanying dispersal and isolation, and the existing histories and archives that painted lesbians with deviance or erased them entirely. The collectives featured in this book are discontinuously tied by their turn to *historiography*, broadly conceived, as an activist approach to shaping communities and changing present and future circumstances—even as they realize the "writing" of history through different media, technologies of production, and rhetorical strategies.

The contingent of filmmakers from the 1990s are part of this fitful retroactivist legacy, their filmic compositions of historiography contributing to its ruptures. In the context of New Queer Cinema, resistant queer activism, and queer theory, filmmakers like Barbara Hammer and Cheryl Dunye complicated the recovery logic that underpinned the earlier retroactivist efforts of LHA and the DOB. Hammer, for example, undermined the authenticity of archives that the LHA promoted by quite obviously manipulating archival records. In *History Lessons*, she took existing archival footage and boldly adulterated it. Eleanor Roosevelt's voice is crudely dubbed over in that memorable scene, the content and purpose of her speech changed by Hammer's speaking the word "lesbian" over Roosevelt's word "woman." Roosevelt's original audience of gender-normative women is also adulterated by Hammer, who intercut images of glamorous butch-femme couples and recognizable LHA collective members into the crowd. By altering the archive through clever mash-ups, Hammer retroactively invents evidence to support a vibrant past of lesbians speaking, playing, and loving in public. Through her remediation of existing footage, Hammer challenges the sanctity of archives themselves—which means implicitly disputing the retroactivism of LHA even as this archive is featured in the film. Nothing queer is orderly or cohesive, and that includes the legacy of lesbian retroactivism.

And yet, despite these discontinuities across time, there is evidence that retroactivists' efforts to change available lesbian history *worked*, their contributions superseding the abnormal psychology books that once held monopoly in the public library. While Radclyffe Hall's influential 1928 novel *The Well of Loneliness* showed protagonist Stephen Gordon surreptitiously consuming sexology books from her father's locked bookshelves to learn more about her pathological "inversion," Alison Bechdel's 2006 graphic memoir *Fun Home: A Family Tragicomic* demonstrates that the first book she purchased in her own research about her sexuality was Martin and Lyon's *Lesbian/Woman* (75) (figure 4.1). Retroactivists like LHA, the June L. Mazer Archives (JLMA), and the DOB succeeded in proliferating different archival texts and spaces where bibliophilic women who also loved women could venture to seek information about the identity and desire of lesbians.

Indeed, the 1990s filmmakers in particular proved the efficacy of LHA's retroactivism, as LHA itself became a sort of "figure" in lesbian history to be revered—and spoofed. While Hammer remixes LHA collective member Mabel Hampton into the audience of Eleanor Roosevelt's convention of "lesbians" in *History Lessons* and Carlomusto and colleagues celebrate the LHA collective and archive in much of *Not Just Passing Through*, Cheryl Dunye actually *parodies* LHA in *The Watermelon Woman*. Her historiographer character visits the lesbian separatist "Center for Lesbian Information Technology" (wittily acronymmed "C.L.I.T."), and there the earnest archivist character informs Cheryl that the relevant

Fig. 4.1. Illustration from *Fun Home: A Family Tragicomic*, by Alison Bechdel. *Copyright © 2006 by Alison Bechdel; used by permission of Houghton Mifflin Harcourt Publishing Company; all rights reserved*

materials she seeks are neither filed nor indexed because the organization is "volunteer-run," and she is forbidden to reproduce any photos she finds until she has received approval by consensus from the archive collective. Writing of this scene, Cvetkovich notes that while those "in the know" can easily recognize C.L.I.T. as a parody of LHA, "its humor can also be considered a form of respect and affection" ("In the Archives" 108); the real-life LHA arouses the same allegiance and adoration that draws Cheryl to the (fictional) black movie actor, Fae Richards, she seeks through her research. Through its own and others' retroactivism, LHA has become a destination for pilgrimage, a resource for women with same-sex desire, and a *figure* in the ongoing composition of the past.

Of course, LHA is not merely material available for remediation in filmic compositions, nor is it involved only in collecting artifacts and records. The archive collective has also been involved in their *production.*

Consider the DOB documentary video project sponsored by LHA in 1987. While the feature-length film was never completed, the process of making it produced dozens of hours of oral history with DOB members and leaders as well as the notes and interview questions. While the tapes and interview notes are held at LHA or in off-site storage, the audio and video interviews are now easily accessible online due to their recent digitization by the students of Pratt Institute's library and information sciences program ("Daughters of Bilitis Video Project").[1] But these video and audio sources are not unadulterated. Driven by LHA's own mission of radical inclusivity, the interview questions and recorded responses reveal that LHA was not simply interested in celebrating the DOB, although the documentary was certainly motivated by the significance of the organization. Rather, LHA set out to preserve the DOB in part through the lens of their own concern for racial, gender, class, and sexual diversity.

According to the filmmakers' records housed in LHA, former DOB members responded to questions about, for instance, whether they believed "Del and Phyllis . . . understood themselves to be a *sexual* organization," whether they "really believed that the lesbian could integrate into society . . . as a positive step," how they "dressed at the time" and encouraged other members to "tone down their masculine dress," and how race and class dynamics worked throughout the organization's tenure. These questions reflect LHA's longtime resistance to censorship of women's sexuality, sublimation of same-sex intimacy, restrictive gender norms, and racial or economic homogenization. The subsequent oral histories now preserved in the archive and online are thus filtered through the perspective of LHA, an organization with an abiding concern for inclusivity, sex-positive feminism, and critical race- and class-consciousness.

This review of the discontinuous legacy of retroactivism finds both reverence and remediation in the ways subsequent generations frame the archives of prior retroactivists, demonstrating the endurance *and* malleability of the fruits of their historiographic labor. But these examples also demonstrate an important point about the rhetoricity of archives: the evidence housed and highlighted in archives can be shaped by the archive itself. The organization, mediation, and even production of archival records and artifacts occur in specific rhetorical situations in response to historically located exigencies. The implications of this point should prompt rhetoricians and historians alike to attend critically to the circumstances of the production and preservation of historical evidence.

When and through what means was the record produced, mediated, selected and arranged?

HAS RETROACTIVISM GONE DIGITAL?

The circumstances of evidence's production and preservation is, of course, profoundly impacted by its *medium*. Another thread woven through this book is the significance of the technology of production for the rhetorical possibilities and constraints of a historiographic act. As I argued in the introduction, print, material archivization, and film afford rhetors different orientations toward archives and evidence. Technologies "appeal to us," as Miller argues, and in doing so encourage and constrain certain rhetorical actions ("Foreword" x). When LHA and JLMA weren't involved in the production of records such as the DOB oral history project, their medium of material archivization generally afforded the acts of *collecting and juxtaposing* artifacts and records. Conversely, Hammer's filmic medium afforded the *manipulation* of these materials. Meanwhile, the print medium of the DOB afforded the *second-hand reiteration* of other women's experience since alphabetic conventions of paraphrase and quotation are more endemic to discursive modes than to multimodal and material modes like film and archivization. In each study, the medium both enabled and constrained the contours of the retroactivist act.

The implications of this call to attend to the circumstances and medium of rhetorical acts of historiography become clear when we look to the present and future of retroactivism. The ubiquity of amateur digital composing practices suggests that online new media might be where retroactivism has moved in the contemporary moment. As Gross has demonstrated, lesbian, gay, bisexual, and trans individuals are active producers and consumers of social media, and, as Dan Cohen and Roy Rosenzweig argue in their guide for composing online history, "the web . . . has given a much louder and more public voice to amateur historians." Thus we might expect retroactivism to proliferate through digital platforms. Video, audio, and image editing software and self-publishing platforms such as blogs and video-sharing websites are widely available—with the potential to reach a far greater audience than, for example, LHA could hope to reach in the 1980s with their traveling slide show packed into a Volkswagen.

But the medium and circumstances of digital, online composing practices also appear to profoundly affect the shape of retroactivism in the contemporary moment. Since the 1990s, lesbian, gay, and trans-identified people have used the Internet to locate others for sexual and supportive relationships (Clift; Lazzara) and to form online communities (Barber; Edwards; Gregg). The virtual, rapid communication across any swath of geographic space seems to rely less on the longer history shaped by LHA and tapped by Barbara Hammer. Instead, it seems to build and reinforce community through informally composed, contemporary experience—shared and meant to be discarded after the conversation's completion. In short, digital composing practices may attenuate the sense that one must look *backward* to the long past to shape present community and identity.

Commenting on the apparent recent shift away from turning to the past, Morris and Rawson write in 2014 that they are "not confident that LGBTQ communities, especially of the current generation, are inclined to be interested or invested in queer archives, history, or memory" (85). For Morris and Rawson, contemporary disinterest in the past, or what John Howard calls "social amnesia," is a product of a failed "mnemonic infrastructure and discourse" (85). Despite the successes and endurance of accounts of lesbian pasts composed by the DOB, LHA, JLMA, and filmmakers, these archives and histories may not be where young women with same-sex desire turn today to learn more about their emerging identity. As this book has argued, queer archives are a product of *kairos*, created and remediated in response to historically specific exigencies, and the circumstances of this moment are different from those in the 1970s, when the archives of LHA, JLMA, and *Lesbian/Woman* were composed, and different from those in the 1990s, when filmic lesbian historiography flourished. With marriage equality granted by the Supreme Court and the "Don't Ask Don't Tell" military policy dismantled, we are some distance from the midcentury moment when the language of sexual identification available to the DOB was, at first, "the variant." Certainly, social ostracism, harassment, and violence remain threats to public displays and revelations about same-sex intimacy and nonnormative gender presentation (and may even increase in our fraught political climate), but the *language* of identification—lesbian, gay, bisexual, trans, and queer—is far more entrenched in vernacular and official discourse alike than in earlier historical moments. We are in a different moment, with different circumstances and media of identificatory autodidacticism.

Morris and Rawson argue that more or different "communal 'norms of remembrance'" are needed today to counter the social amnesia that has concealed the fruits of retroactivism from new generations of people with same-sex desire who seek connection and self-definition (85). To conclude this book, I turn now to digital queer archives to consider whether and how communal norms of remembrance are being engaged online. One common medium of the online composition of remembrance is the digital video, including videos proclaiming to young queers that "it gets better" (Phillips, Majkowski), coming-out videos (Alexander and Losh), and video documentation of ongoing lesbian relationships (McBean). Retroactivism may continue in the age of new media through digital *archivization* of video narratives that speak the more recent, personal past. Digital archives look quite different from place-based archives like LHA, but the path from analog print and material archives to digital archives is neither a neat line of progress nor a radical break: it is another contribution to the ongoing "history of discontinuities" that is the history of retroactivism.

The "It Gets Better" Archive: Collecting Videos of the Recent Past

In 2010 Dan Savage, a nationally syndicated sex advice columnist, published a video in response to the suicide of Billy Lucas, a bullied American teen. In the video, Savage and his husband, Terry Miller, promised that "it gets better," recounting their own experiences as the victims of bullying in their youth before sharing their favorite, more recent memories of experiences they never thought possible as teenagers. Within a week, people across the world had made and uploaded two hundred similar videos to the It Gets Better Project (IGBP) and, by the end of 2015, the collection has grown beyond fifty thousand user-generated videos and fifty million views ("What Is the It Gets Better Project?").

In researching the archive of videos, I selected 250 of the newest videos from the collection, finding that the majority (156) of videographers in my sample were white and self-identified as gay men.[2] Lesbian-identified women produced forty-four videos in my sample, while bisexual-identified women produced nineteen, straight-identified women produced five, and transwomen produced seven. The gender diversity of this archive and the dominance of male-identified contributors set it apart from the other archives featured in this book. Indeed, Laurie M. Phillips maintains that gay-identified white men contributing to the project tend to take the position of

> telling viewers of all sexual orientations, gender expressions, and gender identities that their lives will get better. However, videographers likely have little to no personal experience with viewers' multidimensional identities, thus making it possible for their verbiage to be overlooked or outright ignored by the intended audience. (45)

Yet, because of the popularity of the archive and its unique collection of recent queer experience, the project's lesbian-identified voices provide an interesting case study of the state of retroactivism in the contemporary moment.

Individually, the videos are progress narratives: speakers film themselves with their webcams and recount memories of isolation, alienation, and bullying before sharing more recent, happier memories. In producing their memories for the IGBP, most videographers package traumatic experience in terms of its *pastness*. Their personal histories of bullying and harassment—more often than not in high schools and in small towns—are characterized by their being left behind, by their temporal and geographical distance from the speaker's contemporary queer life. Many of the lesbian-, gay-, and bi-identified speakers describe physically moving to bigger cities or to university after high school as the driving force behind their "better" lives, suggesting the socioeconomic advantages of the contributors.

The personal pasts that precede these "better" moments contrast the trauma and joy preserved in LHA, which sets out to keep those pasts current and usable in formation of collective lesbian identification. Tweaking Cvetkovich's assertion that archives of trauma can serve to mobilize identification, the IGBP videos redefine what it means to be an adult queer person: someone who has experienced trauma but *does so no longer*. The traumatic history is claimed and then renounced, a rhetorical move that Tina Majkowski calls an "unfortunate use of queer futurity" (163). These pasts of oppression are cited as evidence that they can be superseded by the future, not forgotten but left behind, lingering in the present only as badges of strength and courage.

As a collection, the videos' retroactivism works against the dominant narrative of the retrograde, hopeless queer. Dustin Bradley Goltz explains that Savage's archive of videos combats the notion that

> [t]he future, for queers, is always "a harder path" of pain and struggle, a homophobic cautionary tale to prevent children from deviating

> from heteronormative trajectories of marriage, child, and inheritance. Discursively, the story has been, "it gets worse, much worse, for the queer." This essentializing master narrative does not specify its condemnation with regards to race, class, nation, or ability. LGBTQ people are people without futures—doomed peoples. (136)

En masse, the videos provide a collection of evidence against this dominant narrative, demonstrating that life *can* get "better."

Savage has been widely critiqued for defining "better" in terms of his own homonormative privilege as a wealthy, white man with a family and a legion of loyal followers, receiving particularly pointed criticism for sharing his favorite memory of walking the streets of Paris with his son. But, as Goltz argues, Savage clearly situates his video as *one* version of "better," his personal version, which is why the sizable and diverse archive of submissions is vitally important to the project. The meaning of "better" is queered by the sheer number and "contradictory multivocality" (Goltz 138) of the videos. From a rhetorical standpoint, the massive archive, in which contributors create and submit their own videos, makes the composition of the collection a "*participatory* process that deepens, extends, and contradicts the term ["better"] as additional voices continue to enter the discussion" (Goltz 138). Other videos besides Savage's suggest that "better" may not mean family and wealth for some people, but it may mean *stronger:* the ability to handle the challenges of queer life more adeptly, rather than the absence of those challenges. As Gabby Rivera declares in her video,

> As a gay woman of color, I just want to let the youth know that it kind of doesn't get better. Like all these straight rich celebrities like whoever . . . they can tell you that it gets better because they got money and I'm gonna be real because I live this life and I'm not rich and I'm brown and I look like probably most of you. First of all, it doesn't get better. What happens is that *you* get stronger. As an adult, you learn how to deal with it, and you learn how to love yourself and just take it for what it is. (Gabby Rivera)

Still other videos suggest that "better" means finding or creating community or progress in legislation for equal access to marriage and the military (Goltz 138).

Despite the difference in medium, Savage's archive of videos has some parallels to the *Lesbian/Woman* archive, the book composed by Martin and Lyon nearly forty years prior. Both the video archive and the book compile and publish the *recent* past. Rather than preserving or remediating records of a longer or extrapersonal past (as LHA and Barbara Hammer did, with the exception of Hammer's autobiographical *Tender Fictions*), the IGBP archive collects, organizes, and distributes records of recent experience. Like Martin and Lyon's *Lesbian/Woman*, the videos derive their rhetorical impact from the sheer volume of similar but subtly different anecdotes. As Goltz explains, the IGBP's "strength emerges through multivocality and internal contradiction, presenting a queer project of writing, rewriting, and reimagining what 'better' might be—actively pushing at the limited and limiting discourses of future" (139).

But, unlike *Lesbian/Woman*'s medium of print, wherein Martin and Lyon strategically paraphrased secondhand the experiences of women with whom they had corresponded, the "vernacular video" medium of the IGBP "affords a personal, direct, intimate element" (Goltz 141). In the videos, there is *visual* evidence that the speaker has survived the challenges of his, her, or their past, with testimony heard directly from the embodied speaker rather than through a proxy like Martin and Lyon. Coming out on video may be less risky now than it was in the age of the DOB, at least from a legal standpoint, since homosexuality was an arrestable offense in the 1950s and 1960s. However, the motivation for the IGBP—extreme bullying and the hopelessness it can engender in young queers—makes coming out on video a courageous move. The courage of public, personal outing reinforces the videos' message to viewers: that it might someday be possible and safe to come out publicly for them too. At the same time, the vastness of the archive provides some anonymity for video makers, who may blend into the multitude.

Unlike *Lesbian/Woman*, this archive is not organized by categories. Instead, like many digital archives, the collection of videos is essentially a database, which can be browsed or searched using possible keywords in the video titles and captions. This function ensures that videos are likely to be found by the niche audiences to which they are addressed. For example, a search for "lesbian" and "theater" or "butch" provides a video made by Carolyn Gage, a playwright, who addresses the video to "all of you lesbians who might be feeling despair about having a career in theater" (Carolyngage1). Gage recounts a memory of her struggle to find acting work early in her career because of her masculine appearance and manner. She then fast-forwards to her recent past and shares that her life has "gotten better" because she became a successful playwright and *wrote* the roles that were not there for her in the decades earlier. Because her video makes her appearance visible, viewers see that Gage has not compromised her gender presentation; instead, she has worked to create opportunities for others like her that she did not have. Gage's narrative nuances Savage's "better" life of gender normativity, wealth, and family.

Because the narratives are in the medium of video and not text, they are not searchable except by the information the contributors choose to provide about themselves in the titles and captions. So while many, if not all, video makers *speak* their names, most do not put their names in the caption or title. By crafting their titles and captions, video makers circumscribe their likely audience and protect a level of anonymity. This ability makes their disclosure more public than *Lesbian/Woman*'s use of pseudonyms for its anecdotal individuals but less public than it would have been if contributors were forced to identify themselves in the searchable text, which might then appear in a search engine. While nothing is safe on the Internet, the It Gets Better archive builds in some provisions of protection for its contributors. Ultimately, the It Gets Better archive updates but reflects earlier forms of retroactivism I have traced in this book. The video archive becomes discontinuously linked in the legacy of retroactivism through its similarities to strategies employed by the DOB, even as it eschews the remediation of the longer past employed by other retroactivist rhetors.

Coming Out on YouTube: Shaping, and Commodifying, Identification

Similar to the recent-experience video narratives proclaiming that it gets better, the coming-out narrative has become a common genre of lesbian and gay video composition on YouTube. In contrast to the IGBP genre, in which videographers describe and then distance themselves from a traumatic past, the coming-out video genre often shares hints from childhood that support the speaker's assertion of enduring sexual identity. Jonathan Alexander and Elizabeth Losh studied thousands of these coming-out videos for their generic features, finding that the videos often take the form of a "self contained, recognizable, predictable story":

a "journey of assembling clues to personal sexuality that goes back to early experiences" (Alexander and Losh 39). In a coming-out video that has received 1.4 million views, Lucy, a British teen, shares that "all my life I had known there was something not quite right, but I could never really pinpoint what that was. I was 15 or 16, that's usually the age all your friends are interested in boys, it struck me that I wasn't really interested" (Kaelynandlucy, "Lucy: My Coming Out Story"). The past experience is used to support the claim "I am gay" before the speaker shares her experience of telling her friends and family. In her video, Lucy shares the difficulty and anxiety she felt about coming out to her friends and family, her methods (she patched together lines from letters she found online in her e-mail to her parents), and her happiness in her relationship with her then-girlfriend. Like the IGBP archive, these videos provide their videographers with the opportunity to come out publicly, with some protection from a field so flooded with videos that theirs is unlikely to go viral or attract singular attention like Lucy's.

Wishing to gain more views, some viewers have capitalized on YouTube's "video response" function, which links together original videos and other individuals' video responses. This is a way of creating a mini-archive within the millions of videos on YouTube. Alexander and Losh found that one YouTube user, GDProphetXVII, received so many responses to his coming-out video from viewers seeking more advice on how to come out to their own family and friends that he began to archive the videos. He did so by asking other coming-out composers to "video respond" to his own "Coming Out Archive" (GDProphetXVII). That way, when users find his video, they also find many more narratives linked to his own, creating a cache that "might help someone come out for themselves" (GDProphetXVII qtd. in Alexander and Losh 33). These videos ultimately have a different retroactivist purpose than the It Gets Better archive. Rather than recount traumatic experience to connect with viewers and teach them to have hope for a better future, this archive recounts videographers' experience with coming out in order to teach viewers how to come out to their own friends and family.

But, at the same time, the archive may also teach viewers what it means to be gay, reifying static sexual identifications by shaping individuals' experience in its generic form. The genre of the coming-out video encourages video makers to look for clues from their youth that explain their present sexual identification as a way to reinforce the seriousness and staying power of their sexuality against friends and family who might charge (or hope) that it is just an experimental phase. Alexander and Losh's study showed that these clues were more often than not stereotypically gay qualities, for "although the ideal cybersubject as fluid and the ideal queer subject as fluid converge in fictions [about cyberspace] . . . there is more evidence to suggest that online queer communities are stratified into fixed identity hierarchies" (O'Riordan qtd. in Alexander and Losh 44).

Kate O'Riordan suggests that these fixed identity hierarchies may actually be reinforced online because of the commercial functions of the Internet. The reification of marketable categories of identity help shape niche audiences to target. In contrast to the resolutely separatist funding for LHA, for example, online platforms for sharing experience are often means for collecting information for targeted marketing. Coming-out videos hosted on YouTube are housed in a corporate-controlled environment, their retroactivism distinct from LHA's enduring philosophy of independence from institutions.

Transnational Intimacy on YouTube: Documenting Enduring Relationships

While the IGBP and coming-out video archives contain contributions from individuals who speak narratives of their own experience, another genre of video documentation has begun to flourish on YouTube: the ongoing, long-distance lesbian relationship. Couples such as "Jordan and Amanda," "Cydney and Stacey," and "Kaelyn and Lucy" have become "part of a community of lesbian long distance couples on YouTube" who make videos to document the time they share (McBean 283). Kaelyn and Lucy[3] in particular (sometimes called "Luclyn") have their own YouTube channel with almost 250,000 subscribers and thirty million views (Kaelynandlucy, "Kaelyn and Lucy").

As Sam McBean explains, the couple's videos "document each visit they have had together, meaning that as a whole, the videos seemingly not only archive their individual trips but the entirety of the time that they have spent together" (288). To do so, the videos often "montage" experiences the couple share in their visits, beginning with their reunions at the airport, moving through domestic scenes of talking, teasing, eating, and cuddling, and concluding with a reflection on the visit with expressions of love and tears. Lucy is a filmmaker, so the videos are well edited and cinematic, with soundtracks from popular songs. McBean argues that Kaelyn and Lucy's videos draw on cinematographic techniques from romantic Hollywood films, in which montages suggest growing intimacy between a couple.

The couple claims they "started this channel originally as a way to document the precious moments we got to spend together when we were still living apart," as a way to record and relive their rare shared experiences (Kaelynandlucy, "About"). But soon the channel's audience expanded as their videos gained more and more viewers. Commenters, whose remarks below the videos suggest that their (virtual) identities range widely in sexuality, gender, age, race, and nationality, frequently express their emotional connection to the couple: "I.CANT.HOLD.ALL.THESE.FEELS" or "I teared up when you guys hug. I LOVE YOU SO MUCH <3" being typical comments (McBean 283). The couple's distance, anticipation, and reunion drew followers into their romance. McBean contends that this "digital archive of feelings" documents the intimacy of this couple's relationship but also "exceeds and reaches beyond lesbian identification and community" (295). Hosted on YouTube, the couple's relationship is documented, edited into its mediated, montaged form, and delivered to a far more diverse audience than other, intentionally separatist archives featured in this book. At the same time, this digital archive of feelings is also less intentionally retroactivist. The community of long-distance lesbian couples who "vlog" are invested not in shaping lesbian identity or advocating for acceptance or social change but in preserving and celebrating their own relationships, which struggle with distance, and in showing others how long-distance relationships can be successfully navigated. Indeed, many of the comments identify not with the couple's *same-sex* love but with their geographical distance from each other (for instance, an apparently female-identified commenter named Sophie wrote that she is "in a long distance relationship with my boyfriend and you both made me realise how easy it can be!") (qtd in McBean 291).

Yet, while Kaelyn and Lucy's intentions may not be retroactivist, their effect might be. Like Bunny MacCulloch's relationship photo albums, housed in JLMA, these video montages provide visible evidence of lasting lesbian love. Here, as in MacCulloch's decade of photos documenting her everyday experiences with Rita Charette in the 1950s and 1960s, ongoing video updates provide proof of the endurance of intimacy—even across the obstacle of distance. This lasting *intimacy* is what followers and commenters feel attached to, not the gender of videographers' objects of desire. That intimacy was maintained even after Kaelyn and Lucy posted a tearful video in September 2016 announcing their breakup after more than six years together; commenter Carly Rogers posted under the video that "my husband and I have also decided to call it quits. We also had a good run 7 years [*sic*]. But unfortunately sometimes love is temporary.... I wish you both the best. I hope you both have amazing friends and family to help get you through the hard times." Like Sophie, Carly identified not with the gender of the couple but with their love and then their loss.

The Rhetoricity of Video Archives

This brief survey of video archives suggests that the curating of lesbian experience continues online in the digital archivization of video narratives of the recent past, even though these experiences exist among a more diverse spectrum of participants' gender and sexuality and are often dwarfed by the greater numbers of contributions by gay male videographers. As these examples demonstrate, there persists a driving concern to *archive:* to record, collect, arrange, and share past experience for present political and identificatory uses and effects. Like the collectives featured in the chapters of this book, these video archives have a rhetorical purpose. The IGBP is an activist campaign against hopelessness, suicide, and bullying. YouTube coming-out videos are part of an unorganized movement to help lesbian, gay, bisexual, and queer people learn to share their sexuality with their friends and families, though the archive may also have the effect of reifying static sexual identifications. Long-distance lesbian couples document their anticipation and reunions, providing evidence of lasting same-sex love. These are historiographic compositional acts; through them, experience is recorded and archived, there to be *used* to shape a sense of collectivity—as long as the sites are live and the webmasters allow it.

But online new media also appears to change the nature of retroactivism in some fundamental ways. While previous generations of retroactivism were certainly participatory, the immediacy and dispersion of the Internet creates very different forms of community and communication. The nature of online media makes communication more networked and horizontal, less hierarchical. The YouTube archives in particular are continually constructed in a grassroots fashion, without organizational leaders like Martin, Lyon, and Nestle nor individual artists like Hammer and Dunye making representational decisions about the shape of lesbian history.

But the organic emergence of some of these video archives does not mean they are not shaped and curated. Savage's first IGBP video influenced the shape of those to follow, and the coming-out video of YouTube "archivist" GDProphetXVII influenced the video responses he received. Contributions to each of the video archives discussed here are contoured by the genre of the video narratives already populating the archives—genres that may encourage narratives of progress, the search for (and potential invention of) childhood clues, and fixed sexual identification. And, in contrast to some of LHA's explicitly sexual holdings and some of Barbara Hammer's more taboo sexual images, YouTube's rules prohibiting explicit images constrain which versions of sexuality are preserved. Archived video pasts, like other forms of retroactivism, are shaped by their exigencies, audience, and medium.

This reflection suggests that more attention should be paid to amateur historiography in digital media. Like prior retroactivists, creators of digital archives make strategic use of their contents. These archives are designed for specific purposes, and it makes sense to ask who is curating them and to what end, since they provide both identificatory and scholarly resources. When considering digital historiography and archivization, it seems even more important to begin with collectivity and pastness as *questions* rather than givens.

For instance, the DOB cohered in collectivity around middle-class values and the goal of social assimilation, while LHA sought to break down the boundaries of race and class through a radically inclusive policy of seeking out the records of working-class, nonwhite, international, and regional women with same-sex desire. But what happens to the boundaries of class, race, and nation in online retroactivism? The brief survey of digital video archives above suggests that while white gay men have made up the bulk of contributors, the archives include contributions from broad swaths of orientations, ethnicities, gender identities, nationalities, and economic positions. What then is the nature of collectivity in digital arenas where certain demographics remain dominant yet niche contributions (like the video for butches in the theater by Carolyngagel) can be easily located and accessed by viewers seeking specific recognition and guidance? In digital archives, it seems, the figurative language of "the center" and "the margins" no longer quite expresses the relationship between identities nor the way their mediation is accessed.

Related to the shifting nature of collectivity and difference is the question, what is the nature of the past that is constructed and curated online? If digital videos have become new "communal 'norms of remembrance'"

(Morris and Rawson 85) that attenuate the need to look to the long past for identification and political leverage, what is lost beyond nostalgia for earlier norms of remembrance? The digital videos surveyed here seem designed to help other (often young) people navigate the challenges of nonnormative desire, so they are certainly "other-directed" (Glascott); at the same time, however, they are profoundly "self-directed"—a product of the affordances of social media to capture and broadcast the self, often from the privacy of a webcam and a bedroom.

By finding community horizontally—across geographic but not temporal distance—there is a danger that Nestle's aspiration in the epigraph to this book's prologue will cease to be realized. On behalf of LHA, Nestle wished in 1998 that the "discussion of lesbian strategies and identities" represented by the archive's eclectic contents would "go on for generations to come, each decade adding its layer of complexity" ("Will," 1998 233). Nestle's *additive* hope for "the fullest record we can leave" may not be met by online archives of videos that forget the longer past of courageous activism, organizing, intimacies, and gender expressions. The preservation of digital videos for future generations may also be in peril, subject to the whims of the videographer and the webmaster, and so their availability to "diverse and embattled lesbian communities of the future" (Nestle, "Will" 233) cannot be ensured. The future task of retroactivism may be to challenge, or exploit, the ephemeral, corporately controlled, and individual versions of the recent past afforded by online digital media: to "make" the kinds of histories and people necessitated by whichever *kairos* the future encounters.

HOW WILL THE PAST LINGER?

Yet, despite online-video historiography's suppression of the long past, we must also remember that pasts are not always easily silenced. Sometimes the past lingers in ways that are felt in the body, in the heart.[4] Extending Derrida's notion of "hauntology," queer historian Carla Freccero urges us to consider how "affective force of the past in the present" issues forth "desire . . . from another time" (Dinshaw et al. 184). In the context of retroactivism, Freccero's application of hauntology suggests that it is not only rhetors in the present who compose and leverage the past; the past may also haunt the present with buried desires and affects. Sometimes it is loss and absence and trauma itself that are inherited, and because humanity possesses a "general hunger to reabsorb and repress loss" (Rody, "Toni Morrison's *Beloved*" 112), we collude in hushing its affective call. This is why, for Freccero, queer historians have an ethical imperative to listen to the ghosts who linger (*Queer/early/modern* 87).

Taking Freccero's imperative seriously means thinking more deeply about the rhetoricity of the past-present relation: about who speaks, who listens, and when. Ballif offers a robust contribution here, bringing Derridean hauntology to bear on how spectral dialogue across time complicates the shape of the address. For Ballif, "hauntological historiography performs a certain uncertain writing habit in that the historiographer can never know who is addressing whom—nor know the difference between addressor and addressee" ("Historiography as Hauntology" 141). When we listen to ghosts, we invite affects of restlessness, uncertainty, and discomfort; we invite the "indeterminate" ghosts to "render *ourselves* unfamiliar (as scholars and as a discipline)" ("Historiography as Hauntology" 140)—and, I would extend, as gendered and sexual subjects within and outside the academy. Thus, as we think ahead to the future of retroactivism, we must also complicate how we understand the leverage of the past, not only *by* rhetors in the present but also by the past's own affective volition.

Reconsidering collectivity, pastness, and the hauntological rhetorical situation raises more questions than answers about future directions in the study and practice of retroactivism. Yet it may be right to close this book with such openness, for as Nestle wrote recently, her reflections on queer archiving have only generated "new questions, new uncertainties about what we thought it all meant and what the future seems to be about" ("Who Were We" 241). Worried less now about historical erasure, she suggests that the queer archive's own mistakes, omissions, and negotiations between classifying and complicating identity might be what comes to haunt us. Nestle writes,

> [S]ome of the most important collections in the LHA to me are the documents of our failures, of our own exclusions, of the complex face of gender and sexual differences. Queer archives of the future perhaps will give evidence that it is harder to live with a history than without one. (Nestle, "Who Were We" 241)

NOTES

WORKS CITED

INDEX

NOTES

Introduction: Rhetoric and Identification in Grassroots Historiography

1. Bravmann's focus is on the uses of queer history for academics situated in lesbian and gay studies rather than grassroots historiography. Despite claims to attend to "lesbian and gay studies *and* communities—their insistent engagement with history," Bravmann devotes his analysis to historians such as George Chauncey, Esther Newton, Lillian Faderman, Elizabeth Kennedy and Madeline Davis, Allen Berube, and John D'Emilio.

2. As Kyle Jensen maintains, what I call "historiography" could instead be described as "myth," as he argues that Burkean identification owes far more to myth than is typically assumed, that myth creates the conditions of identification to be understood as such.

3. Burke argued that Samson became the "seer" when he collapsed the temple on himself and three thousand Philistines-qua-Royalists, and they became "sightless" (*Rhetoric* 4).

4. Like Burke, Williams parses the relationship between individuals and collectives, claiming provocatively that "the principle we need to break through to new meanings is that of the fundamental relation between organism and organization," neither of which are fixed. "To know ourselves and our world," he contends, we need to continually break down the organism and the organization to the "actual processes which are changing us and which we wish to change" (98).

5. As Glenn explains, "whether using Corbett's, Kennedy's, Kinneavy's, or Murphy's map, we followed an aristocratic blue line, a master narrative that started with Corax and Tisias and led directly to Plato and Aristotle, then Cicero, Quintillian, and St. Augustine, and eventually to Weaver, Richards, Perelman, and Burke" ("Remapping" 287).

6. This intervention comes in a long line of reflexive critique. One defining characteristic of feminist historiography is the willingness to think reflectively

and critically about our own methodological shortcomings. For instance, Carol Mattingly questioned feminist historiography's tendency to recover historical figures—such as elite, white suffragettes like Elizabeth Cady Stanton and Susan B. Anthony—who reminded contemporary academic feminists of themselves or their values, resulting in a canonization of *particular* women. Thus the move toward inclusivity that began as an effort to diversify the history of rhetoric by adding women to the cacophony of male voices began to diversify the category of women as well. For example, Shirley Wilson Logan's 1995 book *With Pen and Voice: A Critical Anthology of Nineteenth Century African-American Women* recovered the voices and rhetoric of African American women into the history of rhetoric, to provide a storehouse of African American women's discourse so that it could be heard and studied.

7. For an interesting example of this kind of work, see Lindal Buchanan's *Regendering Delivery*, which examines how women in the 19th century leveraged their maternalized gender expression to, paradoxically and rebelliously, speak publicly.

8. Likewise, prominent queer theorists such as Lee Edelman, Eve Kasofsky Sedgwick, and Leo Bersani often take literary representations of gay men as their primary texts, contributing to a sense that "queer studies" equates with white gay men, as Halberstam acknowledges and critiques in "Shame and White Gay Masculinity."

1. The Daughters of Bilitis Archive: Clearing Historical Space for Clustered Anecdotes

1. These letters were received between 1972 and 1979 and are now part of the Phyllis Lyon and Del Martin Papers at San Francisco's GLBT Historical Society.

2. Despite its infamy as a "wide-open" city, 1950s San Francisco was also subject to Joseph McCarthy's drive to rid the country of communism and any evidence of internal decay. Femininity and homosexuality became symbols of weakness and vulnerability, while nuclear family ideals of patriarchal leadership and heterosexual monogamy (at least by women) were lauded in both official and vernacular discourse. As Boyd explains, homosexuality became ideologically fused with other sins that defied social control, such as prostitution and juvenile delinquency, an association that played out in the reality of the bar scene. The conflation of homosexuality with immorality, prostitution, and drug use produced widely disseminated stereotypes of lesbians as dangerous delinquents and resulted in severe police aggression and social ostracism.

3. Boyd chronicles the gender transgressive and working-class culture of queer bars in San Francisco, arguing that the "roots of queer activism are

. . . found in the less organized (but numerically stronger) pockets of queer association and camaraderie in bars and taverns" (10). She unearths an entwined history of sex tourism (voyeuristic tourists interested in witnessing cross-dressing and "same-sex and cross-race sexual display"); prostitution; drag king entertainment; and lesbian culture in the North Shore bars of 1930s–50s San Francisco (15).

4. The split across class and race lines was not conscious at the time; in *Lesbian/Woman*, Martin and Lyon write that "only recently have we realized that the DOB split was along worker/middle class lines" (222).

5. The Mattachine Society and ONE, Inc., were the first organizations in the homophile movement but were primarily run by and for gay male activists. The DOB was formed in part because issues distinct to lesbians were not considered by the movement; the existing organizations focused more on public sex laws than issues like lesbian motherhood and employment rights, for example.

6. This transition is evinced in the DOB statement of purpose, which occurred without editorial comment in the *Ladder*. From the statement's inception through 1966, the first purpose had included (among several other dicta) the phrase, "education of the *variant* . . . by advocating a mode of behavior and dress acceptable to society" (1966, 11.3, 1; my emphasis). The January 1967 issue's first goal reads, "education of the *Lesbian* . . . by providing the Lesbian a forum for the interchange of ideas within her own group" (1967, 11.4, 1; my emphasis). There is some evidence that women with same-sex desire referred to themselves and each other as "gay," but there is little to no use of the term in DOB-composed literature, perhaps in an effort to distinguish themselves from the gay men of One, Inc., and Mattachine.

7. For a longer history of lesbian identification and naming, see Halperin's *How to Do the History of Sexuality*, in which he traces the first usages of "Lesbian" and other classifications of relations between women.

8. While liberal feminism sought legal redress for gender inequality through institutional channels, radical feminism advocated direct action to transform systemic patriarchal structures and values. These branches often conflicted in their methods and targets, but both tended to treat feminist lesbians with hostility, viewing sexuality as a distraction from the goal of gender equality. Seeking recognition from the women's movement, lesbian feminist groups posed lesbianism as "a political strategy that was a logical conclusion of feminism" (Taylor and Whittier 173). *Lesbian/Woman* evinces yet another divergent strand in this context. Focusing neither on legal rights, direct action, nor lesbianism *as* feminism, Martin and Lyon advocated conformance to middle-class values and self-acceptance against isolating discourses of lesbian

pathology, reaching rural lesbians whose letters indicate little participation in or awareness of the more radical movements.

9. Members largely joined feminist efforts rather than gay liberation after the DOB-NACHO convention in 1966 (a joint conference between the DOB and the North American Conference of Homophile Organizations). The conference, which brought together several, primarily gay male, homophile organizations overwhelmingly featured male speakers and issues. After the conference, DOB members began to feel they were more aligned with the burgeoning feminist movement than gay activism (*Lesbian/Woman* 256). *Lesbian/Woman* primarily recounts experiences of women Martin and Lyon had met during the 1950s and 1960s but does reveal its historical moment in the brief, final chapter, a manifesto for lesbian-feminist liberation exhorting readers to eschew toleration and demand acceptance. Interestingly, no readers referenced this chapter in their letters housed in the GLBT Historical Society archive.

10. Ann Aldrich was Marijane Meaker's pseudonym, chosen because it seemed to be a benign American women's name. Meaker wrote under several other pseudonyms as well.

11. Despite the arguably negative representation, many women in the 1950s responded gratefully to Aldrich, appreciating the veritable guidebook to the New York lesbian bar scene that her books provided for women seeking the company of women and having no other recourse to find it. Aldrich received hundreds of letters, apparently mostly positive, from her lesbian readers. She devotes one chapter in *We, Too, Must Love* to reprinting excerpts from the letters of her fans.

12. Gene Damon was the pen name of Barbara Grier, who wrote the literary reviews for the *Ladder* for many years. She also wrote under the pseudonyms Lennox Strong and Vern Niven. In 1968 she became editor of the *Ladder*, expanding its page count to forty glossy pages and removing the word "Lesbian" from the cover in an attempt to reach more women. In 1970, when the DOB disbanded, she and then-DOB president Rita LaPorte, broke into the DOB office, took back issues and the two existing copies of the mailing list, and moved production of the *Ladder* to Reno, Nevada, without informing Martin or Lyon. This amounted to a theft of the magazine, according to Martin and Lyon, because, to assuage the fears of exposure held by subscription holders, there were only the two copies of the mailing list.

13. Their move to oppose and revise professional medical opinions shows a transitioned understanding from the DOB's early days. Initially, the DOB spent much time seeking to participate in "authorized and responsible" psychology and sociology studies to better understand the "variant" (as described in the organization's first published goals). They first sought to work *with*

medical professionals, but through the experience of working with "experts," they concluded that biases blinded researchers from objectively designed studies and interpreted results. Consequently, their longtime research director, Florence Jaffee, designed and interpreted many surveys of the *Ladder* readers, the results of which came to be regularly printed in the newsletter.

14. After *Spring Fire* in 1952, Meaker (Ann Aldrich's real name) would go on to write more than sixteen pulps as Vin Packer.

15. On the inside cover of *Lesbian/Woman*, Martin and Lyon write, "The people in this book are real. The incidents are true. However, we have changed most of the names and places to protect the innocent, lest they be punished for the infamous crime of being." I enclose these names in quotation marks to emphasize their pseudonymic nature.

16. The rurally based women who wrote Martin and Lyon commonly cited feelings of isolation. But, as scholars such as Mary Gray and John Howard have argued, it is important to nuance the metronormative narrative that positions the rural as a space that must be "left behind to reach gay culture and community formation in the cities" (Howard 63). As some letters suggest, some writers did have access to gay bars but avoided them because they felt out of place among the patrons. Connection with other lesbian-identifying women may have been possible in nonurban locations, but these individuals' sense of lesbian identity precluded membership in bar-based community.

17. While Meeker's point is mostly accurate, *Lesbian/Woman* does briefly acknowledge that black lesbians were often forced to "make a choice between the two 'causes' that touched their lives so intimately": civil and gay rights (114). This realization in 1972 may have come later than the organization's active period in the 1950s and 1960s.

18. Martin and Lyon's contract was terminated also because the editors complained that the authors refused to admit any doubt about their "choice of lifestyle," when "it's the nature of being human to have doubts." But Martin and Lyon would not suggest that lesbianism might be a moral, mental, or physical illness, even if their contract would be terminated as a result. Because they were promoting a collective self-acceptance, they attributed the problems lesbians suffered to the hostility of society, not lesbians themselves.

19. San Francisco's Glide Publications picked up the book.

20. Though I pose this question to queer archives, it has been asked of queer history more generally by theorists such as Thomas Piontek, who critiques the narratives that set the 1969 Stonewall Inn uprising as the origin of gay activism and community and thereby discount and reduce earlier homophile efforts. Queer theory's opposition to contemporary forms of homonormativity makes it difficult to place earlier forms of proto-homonormative activism.

2. *Classifying Collections: Subversive Schemas as* Topoi *in Place-Based Archives*

1. Fonfa wrote, "Since [LHA], many local projects have formed and community archives are now in Florida, Washington DC, Illinois, Kentucky, Tennessee, Georgia, Massachusetts, and most recently, a Third World Women's Archives with lesbian materials in Connecticut" (Bunny MacCulloch Papers, 1982–84 WCLC Ads and Newsletters, June L. Mazer Archives at UCLA).

2. The New Alexandria Archive eventually moved to its current home in Northampton, Massachusetts, where it was renamed the Sexual Minorities Archive by archivist Bet Power, broadening its scope considerably from a separatist lesbian archive to one that celebrates the diverse genders and sexualities that are and are not represented by the "LGBTQ" acronym (Hemmings 45). For an in-depth study of this archive and its archivist, Bet Power, see also Rawson's 2010 doctoral dissertation, "Archiving Transgender: Affects, Logics, and the Power of Queer History."

3. This separatism distinguishes the archive from the ONE National Gay and Lesbian Archives and from San Francisco's GLBT Historical Society, founded in 1985.

4. Mazer and MacCulloch collaborated with the large lesbian organization Southern California Women for Understanding (1975–99) and the Latina lesbian woman's center Connexxus (1984–90) to move the archives to Los Angeles.

5. The damaging affective impact of available library research was a significant focus of the anecdotes clustered in Martin and Lyon's *Lesbian/Woman*.

6. Other lesbian archives, like Chicago's New Alexandria Library (which later became the Sexual Minorities Archive), were just as aware that lesbians were destroying their own records. Like LHA and JLMA, this archive had to convince women to save their writings and artifacts. In an interview with Clare Hemmings, founder Bet Power recalled that "it took a while for the communities to understand that the way to build identity is to preserve records. The biggest thing to get over was internalized phobia . . . a lot of individuals didn't see their own papers as having worth and value to contribute or save. And so you'd get these tremendous collections of love letters that were burned or thrown out . . ." (qtd in Hemmings "From Lesbian Nation to Transgender Liberation" 45, "Bisexual," Subject Files, Lesbian Herstory Archives).

7. The publishing of this principle in the sixteenth newsletter marks a change from previous newsletters. The first newsletter, published in 1975, includes a statement of purpose that articulates many of the enduring principles—

the goal of preserving lesbian life and activities for future generations against patriarchal and homophobic historiographic practices; government by a lesbian collective; acquisitions of any materials possessed and/or produced by a lesbian woman. But in this inaugural newsletter, "lesbian" is not defined. The original statement of purpose reappears, mostly consistently, in subsequent newsletters until 1986, when it is omitted for the next 10 years. Its reappearance in the 1996 newsletter, revised to define "lesbian" as any woman who "has had the courage to touch or desire another woman" suggests that issues of definition may have bubbled behind the scenes of LHA's public documents.

8. LHA contains several other examples of synecdoche through repetition. The pulp paperback's illustrated covers are reproduced for a periodic exhibit called "Queer Covers: Lesbian Survival Literature" and also featured in the slide shows. One particularly important book, Radclyffe Hall's *The Well of Loneliness*, is represented in the slide show, as well as several newsletters, and in surveys querying women about their experiences receiving the book and its importance in their lives

9. The many oral history interviews have been digitized from VHS format by students in the Pratt Institute's Library and Information Science Program. LHA now links to the Daughters of Bilitis Video Project on their website, providing access to rough cuts of portions of the unreleased documentary as well as to video interviews ("Digital Collections").

3. Remediating the Archive: Documentary Compositions of Lesbian Pasts

1. Biren's films included *For Love and for Life* (1988), a documentary of the 1987 March on Washington for Lesbian and Gay Rights; *A Simple Matter of Justice* (1993), a documentary of the 1993 March on Washington for Lesbian and Gay Rights; and *No Secret Anymore* (2003), a documentary on Del Martin and Phyllis Lyon, founders of the Daughters of Bilitis.

2. My attention to films as compositions that employ multimodal rhetorical strategies has precedence in both new media and rhetoric and composition studies. For example, Lev Manovich writes in *The Language of New Media* that "the printed word tradition that initially dominated the language of cultural interfaces is becoming less important, while the part played by *cinematic elements* is becoming progressively stronger. This is consistent with a general trend in modern society toward presenting more and more information in the form of *time-based audiovisual moving image sequences* rather than as [static] text" (78, emphasis mine). Murray calls cinema the "logical conclusion" of current trends in rhetoric and composition, arguing that "not only is rhetoric based in multiple modes, it is also the case that we are headed for an intellectual environment that will privilege multiple modes composed *in time* as

in cinema" (182). Likewise Jeff Rice argues for a "media-directed approach" to composing that "view[s] film as another source of rhetorical expression for study and output" (78).

3. Films like Jennie Livingston's 1990 *Paris Is Burning*, Todd Haynes's 1991 *Poison*, and Todd Kalin's 1992 *Swoon* achieved success at Sundance and other festivals.

4. "The New Queer Cinema" was published in the *Village Voice* in March 1992, while Hammer's first lesbian historiography documentary was first shown at the Toronto Film Festival in September of that year. Dunye's film *The Watermelon Woman* was featured in Rich's 2013 booklength treatment of New Queer Cinema, but Hammer remained positioned as an early pioneer, the book citing only her films from the 1970s.

5. For example, Judith Butler features Jennie Livingston's 1990 film *Paris Is Burning* in her classic 1993 text, *Bodies That Matter*.

6. Queer rhetorical scholars' challenge to normative criteria for recovery has roots in a longer feminist tradition led by historians like Joan Wallach Scott, rhetorical historiographers like Biesecker and Ballif, and, of course, Nietsche and Foucault. Indeed, Cloud cites Biesecker's groundbreaking 1992 feminist historiography article, "Coming to Terms with Recent Attempts to Write Women into the History Of Rhetoric," and extends its reproach to the liberal recovery of queer subjects, contending like Biesecker that the "project of liberal recovery risks replicating an unhelpful ideological individualism that fails to recognize the structural contexts of and possibilities for queer subjects to emerge" (Cloud 25).

7. Most of these films were first released internationally at general film festivals like the Berlin International and Sundance Film Festivals and at gay and lesbian film festivals, such as Outfest (Los Angeles) and Frameline (San Francisco). Queer film festivals create a unique rhetorical context in which a majority queer audience gathers in a time and place to view films typically produced by queer filmmakers about queer subjects. Filmmaker Bill Basquin describes how queer festivals provide a "feeling of communion" among the audience rather than "just the pleasurable experience of watching a good movie" (124). Following Jennifer Worley, Basquin calls the all-ages spaces sites of "queer reproduction," a place where viewers learn about queerness and even learn to be queer filmmakers. Showings are regularly followed by question-and-answer sessions with filmmakers, facilitating interaction between the viewers and the composers. Another filmmaker, Q. Allan Brocka, describes queer festivals like this: "no matter where [in the world], once you get into a theater full of queer people . . . even if they hate it, they're still there and there's a reason to be there with the crowd and to see something of yourself in the film" (125). Perhaps for this reason, Olivier Ducastel and

Jacques Martineau remark that viewers self-select along gendered lines which films they choose to see, commenting on the "total absence of guys during the screening of lesbian films, while the gals are more curious about the gay male films" (134). So, even though lesbian and gay film *festivals* are almost universally mixed in gender and sexual orientation, audiences of individual films—at least those produced by and about lesbians—are often segregated by gender, contributing a sense of separatist community in the rhetorical context. After the festival, the films are made available for purchase from distributors such as Women Make Movies or through the filmmakers' personal websites. Because of the expense of marketing and individual DVDs, festivals may provide the largest audience of lesbian viewers the filmmakers can hope to reach.

8. Hammer's representation of memory reflects David Lowenthal's contention that we "select, distill, distort, and transform the past, accommodating things remembered to the needs of the present. . . . Memories are not ready-made reflections of the past, but eclectic selective reconstructions based on subsequent actions and perceptions and on ever-changing codes by which we delineate, symbolize and classify the world around us" (210). Hammer admits and even emphasizes the mediation of her memory, the way in which her experiences are reconfigured by her "subsequent actions and perceptions"—her subsequent identification as a lesbian, the "ever changing codes" through which she organizes herself within a network of communities.

9. This strategy was also used in other films in the New Queer Cinema wave. Cecilia Barriga's short film *Meeting of Two Queens* (1991), takes archival footage of Greta Garbo and Marlene Dietrich and edits it together in an experimental film to suggest their characters' desire for one another. Like Roosevelt, Garbo and Dietrich were rumored to have had an affair in 1925, according to Diana McLellan's *The Girls: Sappho Goes to Hollywood.*

10. For histories suggesting Roosevelt's "lesbianism," see works by Blanche Wiesen Cook (*Eleanor Roosevelt*, vol. 1, 1993), Neil Miller (*Out of the Past: Gay and Lesbian History from 1869 to the Present*, 2008), and Rodger Streitmatter (*Empty without You: The Intimate Letters of Eleanor Roosevelt and Lorena Hickok*, 2000). See also Dana Cloud's "The First Lady's Privates" in *Queering Public Address* for a critique of moves to either claim or deny Roosevelt into "lesbian history."

11. Mash-ups like these are another example of multimodal nonlinearity. By mashing together clips from different periods, Hammer undermines linear chronology, any sense of a causal temporal march that might lead a particular present.

12. When Hammer could not gain access to an archived film reel, either because of copyright or because, for example, a newspaper tabloid story did

not have a film equivalent, she employed actors to perform what "would have been" archival footage. For instance, intercut with images of a tabloid headline about lesbians "nabbed for armed robbery," Hammer films New York drag kings acting out a mob scene in the streets. In another filmed scene, Hammer has actors play a doctor, a femme patient, and the patient's butch partner. The doctor, played by gay composer David del Tredici, tries to measure the patient's lesbian anatomical difference, implicitly referring to the sexological studies of the late nineteenth century. But in a twist, Hammer has the patient (art critic Coco Fusco) and her lover (artist Jane Fine) turn the measuring tool on the doctor, pinning him down and assessing his masculinity.

13. Hammer includes footage of an 1896 snuff film featuring a woman being hung. She has no evidence that the woman in the film was hung because she was a lesbian, but she assumes that such violence was perpetrated against lesbians, or against women whose desire in some way exceeded demands for feminine chastity. In an interview, Hammer speculates on the woman's identity: "Maybe she's a prostitute, maybe she was strictly sexual and erotic, maybe she was just your run-of-the-mill lesbian witch! But we do know that lesbians were murdered for their sexual principles throughout the ages, in all different kind of ways. So she stands as a marker of lesbian persecution" (Handelman and Hammer).

4. "A History of Discontinuities": On the Past and Future of Retroactivism

1. The tapes are filed in the audiovisual collection at LHA, while the notes and records of the filmmaking process are filed in the archival collection.

2. This sample of videos was taken in August 2014.

3. Lucy is the same British teen who made the popular coming-out video cited by Alexander and Losh, while Kaelyn lived in the United States.

4. As one example of the past's affective interference in the present, literary critic Caroline Rody investigates the psychic inheritance of slavery: "the 'interior' place in the African-American psyche where a slave's face still haunts," that "excess of African-American history" that defies language and is "known in the bones and yet not at all" (97–99).

WORKS CITED

Aaron, Michele, ed. *New Queer Cinema: A Critical Reader.* New Brunswick, NJ: Rutgers UP, 2004. Print.

Abbott, Sidney, and Barbara J. Love. *Sappho Was a Right-On Woman: A Liberated View of Lesbianism.* New York: Stein and Day, 1972. Print.

Adler, Melissa. "Transcending Library Catalogs: A Comparative Study of Controlled Terms in Library of Congress Subject Headings and User-Generated Tags in LibraryThing for Transgender Books." *Journal of Web Librarianship* 3.4 (2009): 309–31. Web.

Aldrich, Ann. *We, Too, Must Love.* Greenwich, CT: Fawcett Publications, 1958. Print.

———. *We Walk Alone.* Greenwich, CT: Fawcett Publications, 1955. Print.

Alexander, Jonathan, and Elizabeth Losh. "'A YouTube of One's Own?': 'Coming Out' Videos as Rhetorical Action." Pullen and Cooper 37–50.

Alexander, Jonathan, and Jacqueline Rhodes. "Queer Rhetoric and the Pleasures of the Archive." *Enculturation.* N.p. 16 Jan. 2012. Web. 9 Apr. 2013.

Archives of the Archives Files. Lesbian Herstory Archives.

Ballif, Michelle. "Historiography as Hauntology: Paranormal Investigations into the History of Rhetoric." Ballif, *Theorizing* 139–53.

———. "Introductory Notes from the Editor: Untimely Historiographies." *Rhetoric Society Quarterly* 44.3 (2014): 201–3. Web.

———. "Re/dressing Histories; or, On Re/covering Figures Who Have Been Laid Bare by Our Gaze." *Rhetoric Society Quarterly* 22.1 (1992): 91–98. Print.

———, ed. *Theorizing Histories of Rhetoric.* Carbondale: Southern Illinois UP, 2014. Print.

Barber, Trudy. "Stephanie Is Wired: Who Shall Turn Him On?" Pullen and Cooper 245–57.

Baron, Jaimie. *The Archive Effect: Found Footage and the Audiovisual Experience of History.* London: Routledge, 2014. Print.

Basquin, Bill. "A Site for Queer Reproduction." *GLQ: A Journal of Lesbian and Gay Studies* 14.1 (2008): 122–24. Print.

Bechdel, Alison. *Fun Home: A Family Tragicomic*. Boston: Houghton Mifflin, 2006. Print.

Bersani, Leo. *Homos*. Cambridge, MA: Harvard UP, 1995. Print.

Bessette, Jean. "An Archive of Anecdotes: Raising Lesbian Consciousness after the Daughters of Bilitis." *Rhetoric Society Quarterly* 43.1 (2013): 22–45. Print.

———. "Queer Rhetoric in Situ." *Rhetoric Review* 35.2 (2016): 148–64. Web.

Biesecker, Barbara A. "Coming to Terms with Recent Attempts to Write Women into the History of Rhetoric." *Philosophy and Rhetoric* 25 (1992): 140–61. Print.

———. "Of Historicity, Rhetoric: The Archive as Scene of Invention." *Rhetoric and Public Affairs* 9.1 (2006): 124–31. Print.

Bisexual. Subject Files. Lesbian Herstory Archives.

Bolter, J. David, and Richard A. Grusin. *Remediation: Understanding New Media*. Cambridge, MA: MIT, 1999. Print.

Booth, Mark. "'Campe-Toi!': On the Origins and Definitions of Camp." Cleto, *Camp* 66–79.

Boyd, Nan Alamilla. *Wide-Open Town: A History of Queer San Francisco to 1965*. Berkeley: U of California P, 2003. Print.

Bravmann, Scott. *Queer Fictions of the Past: History, Culture, and Difference*. Cambridge, UK: Cambridge UP, 1997. Print.

Brocka, Q. Allan. "A Theatre Full of Queer People." *GLQ: A Journal of Lesbian and Gay Studies* 14.1 (2008): 124–26. Web.

Brooke, Collin Gifford. *Lingua Fracta: Toward a Rhetoric of New Media*. Cresskill, NJ: Hampton, 2009. Print.

Buchanan, Lindal. *Regendering Delivery: The Fifth Canon and Antebellum Women Rhetors*. Carbondale: Southern Illinois UP, 2005. Print.

Burke, Kenneth. *A Grammar of Motives*. Berkeley: U of California P, 1969. Print.

———. *A Rhetoric of Motives*. 1950. Berkeley: U of California, 1969. Print.

Butler, Judith. *Bodies That Matter: On the Discursive Limits of "Sex."* New York: Routledge, 1993.

Campbell, Karlyn Kohrs. *Man Cannot Speak for Her*. New York: Greenwood, 1989. Print.

———. "The Rhetoric of Women's Liberation: An Oxymoron." *Communication Studies* 50.2 (1999): 125–37. Print.

Carmichael, James V., ed. *Daring to Find Our Names: The Search for Lesbigay Library History*. Westport, CT: Greenwood, 1998. Print.

Carolyngage1. "It Gets Better . . . for Lesbian Butches!" *YouTube*. 26 Sept. 2010. Web. 12 Nov. 2016.

Certeau, Michel de. *The Writing of History*. New York: Columbia UP, 1988. Print.

The Children's Hour. Dir. William Wyler. Perf. Audrey Hepburn, Shirley MacLaine, and James Garner. MGM, 1961. DVD.

Cleto, Fabio, ed. *Camp: Queer Aesthetics and the Performing Subject; A Reader.* Ann Arbor: U of Michigan P, 1999. Print.

Clift, Joseph. "Healthy Information, STDs, and the Internet: Implications for Gay Men." Pullen and Cooper 258–70.

Cloud, Dana L. "The First Lady's Privates: Queering Eleanor Roosevelt for Public Address Studies." Morris, *Queering* 23–44.

Cohen, Cathy J. "Punks, Bulldaggers, and Welfare Queens: The Radical Potential of Queer Politics?" *GLQ: A Journal of Lesbian and Gay Studies* 3.4 (1997): 437–65. Web.

Cohen, Daniel J., and Roy Rosenzweig. *Digital History: A Guide to Gathering, Preserving, and Presenting the Past on the Web.* Philadelphia: U of Pennsylvania P, 2006. Print.

Cohen, Martin F. "Neighborhood Report: Park Slope; in Lesbian Archive, Education and Sanctuary." *New York Times* 7 Apr. 1996, sec. B: 9. Print.

Cook, Blanche Wiesen. *Eleanor Roosevelt.* New York: Viking, 1993. Print.

Cram, E. "Archival Ambience and Sensory Memory: Generating Queer Intimacies in the Settler Colonial Archive." *Communication and Critical/Cultural Studies* 13.2 (2016): 1–21. Web.

Crimp, Douglas. "Right On, Girlfriend!" *Fear of a Queer Planet: Queer Politics and Social Theory.* Ed. Michael Warner. Minneapolis: U of Minnesota, 1993. 300–320. Print.

Cutter, Charles A., W. P. Cutter, Worthington Chauncey Ford, Philip Lee Phillips, and Oscar George Theodore Sonneck. *Rules for a Dictionary Catalog.* Washington, DC: GPO, 1904. Print.

Cvetkovich, Ann. *An Archive of Feelings: Trauma, Sexuality, and Lesbian Public Cultures.* Durham, NC: Duke UP, 2003. Print.

———. "In the Archives of Lesbian Feelings: Documentary and Popular Culture." *Camera Obscura: Feminism, Culture, and Media Studies* 17.1 (2002): 107–47. Print.

Danbolt, Matthias. "Touching History: Archival Relations in Queer Art and Theory." *Lost and Found: Queerying the Archive.* Ed. Matthias Danbolt, Jane Rowley, and Louise Wolthers. Copenhagen: Kunsthallen Nikolaj, 2009. 27–54. Print.

"Daughters of Bilitis Video Project." *Omeka RSS.* Lesbian Herstory Archives and Pratt Institute's Library and Information Sciences Program. Web. 23 Nov. 2016. http://herstories.prattinfoschool.nyc/omeka/exhibits/show/daughters-of-bilitis-video-pro.

Davis, Diane. "Identification: Burke and Freud on Who You Are." *Rhetoric Society Quarterly* 38.2 (2008): 123–47. Web.

Davy, Kate. "Cultural Memory and the Lesbian Archive." *Beyond the Archives: Research as a Lived Process.* Ed. Gesa Kirsch and Liz Rohan. Carbondale: Southern Illinois UP, 2008. 128–38. Print.

DeJean, Joan E. *Fictions of Sappho, 1546–1937.* Chicago: U of Chicago P, 1989. Print.

Delagrange, Susan. "Wunderkammer, Cornell, and the Visual Canon of Arrangement." *Kairos* 13.2 (2009). Web.

d'Emilio, John. *Sexual Politics, Sexual Communities.* 2nd ed. Chicago: U of Chicago P, 1998. Print.

Derrida, Jacques. *Archive Fever: A Freudian Impression.* Chicago: U of Chicago P, 1996. Print.

"Digital Collections." *The Lesbian Herstory Archives: Using the Archives.* Web. 12 Nov. 2016.

Dinshaw, Carolyn. *Getting Medieval: Sexualities and Communities, Pre- and Postmodern.* Durham, NC: Duke UP, 1999. Print.

Dinshaw, C., L. Edelman, R. A. Ferguson, C. Freccero, E. Freeman, J. Halberstam, A. Jagose, C. Nealon, and N. T. Hoang. "Theorizing Queer Temporalities: A Roundtable Discussion." *GLQ: A Journal of Lesbian and Gay Studies* 13.2–3 (2007): 177–95. Web.

Douglas, Susan J. *Listening In: Radio and the American Imagination.* Minneapolis: U of Minnesota P, 2004. Print.

Duberman, Martin B., Martha Vicinus, and George Chauncey, eds. *Hidden from History: Reclaiming the Gay and Lesbian Past.* New York: New American Library, 1989. Print.

Dubriwny, Tasha N. "Consciousness-Raising as Collective Rhetoric: The Articulation of Experience in the Redstockings' Abortion Speak-Out of 1969." *Quarterly Journal of Speech* 91.4 (2005): 395–422. Print.

Ducastel, Olivier, and Jacques Martineau. "Very Good For Our Morale." *GLQ: A Journal of Lesbian and Gay Studies* 14.1 (2008): 133–34. Print.

Duggan, Lisa. *Sex Wars: Sexual Dissent and Political Culture.* New York: Routledge, 1995. Print.

———. *The Twilight of Equality? Neoliberalism, Cultural Politics, and the Attack on Democracy.* Boston: Beacon, 2003. Print.

Edel, Deborah. Correspondence with the author. July 2011. E-mail.

Edelman, Lee. *No Future: Queer Theory and the Death Drive.* Durham, NC: Duke UP, 2004. Print.

Edwards, Monica. "Transconversations: New Media, Community, and Identity." Pullen and Cooper 159–72.

Enoch, Jessica. "Releasing Hold: Feminist Historiography without the Tradition." Ballif, *Theorizing* 58–73.

Enoch, Jessica, and Jean Bessette. "Meaningful Engagements: Feminist Historiography and the Digital Humanities." *College Composition and Communication* 64.4 (June 2013): 634–60. Web.

Ester Frances Bentley Papers. June L. Mazer Archives.

The Female Closet. Dir. Barbara Hammer. Barbara Hammer, 1996. DVD.

Five Lesbian Brothers. *Five Lesbian Brothers, Four Plays.* New York, Theatre Communications Group, 2000. Print.

Fonfa, Lynn. "West Coast Lesbian Collections: A Herstorical Wanderground." *Coming Up!* (June 1982), Bunny MacCulloch Papers, June L. Mazer Archives at UCLA.

For Love and for Life: The 1987 March on Washington for Lesbian and Gay Rights. Dir. Joan E. Biren. Frameline, 1988. DVD.

Foucault, Michel. *A History of Sexuality.* Vol. 1. Harmondsworth, UK: Penguin, 1990. Print.

———. "The Historical *a priori* and the Archive." *The Archive.* Ed. Charles Merewether. Cambridge, MA: MIT P, 2006. 26–30. Print.

Freccero, Carla. *Queer/early/modern.* Durham, NC: Duke UP, 2006. Print.

Freeman, Elizabeth. "Introduction." *GLQ: A Journal of Gay and Lesbian Studies* 12.2–3 (2007): 159–76. Web.

———. *Time Binds: Queer Temporalities, Queer Histories.* Durham, NC: Duke UP, 2010. Print.

Freydberg, Elizabeth Hadley. "Review." *The American Historical Review* 100.4 (1995): 1210-212. Web.

Fuss, Diana. *Essentially Speaking: Feminism, Nature and Difference.* London: Routledge, 1990. Print.

Gabby Rivera. "It Gets Better." *YouTube.* 29 Sept. 2010. Web. 12 Nov. 2016. https://www.youtube.com/watch?v=Gr5ix1UUnPI.

GDProphetXVII. "Coming Out Archive." *YouTube.* 24 Oct. 2007. Web. 12 Nov. 2016.

Glascott, Brenda. "Constricting Keywords: Rhetoric and Literacy in Our History Writing." *Literacy in Composition Studies* 1.1 (Mar. 2013). Web. Apr. 2013.

Glenn, Cheryl. "Remapping Rhetorical Territory." *Rhetoric Review* 13.2 (1995): 287–303. Print.

Glenn, Cheryl, and Jessica Enoch. "Invigorating Historiographic Practices in Rhetoric and Composition." *Working in the Archives: Practical Research Methods for Rhetoric and Composition.* Ed. Alexis Ramsey, Wendy Sharer, Barbara L'Eplattenier, and Lisa Mastrangelo. Carbondale: Southern Illinois UP, 2010. 11–27. Print.

Goltz, Dustin Bradley. "It Gets Better: Queer Futures, Critical Frustrations, and Radical Potentials." *Critical Studies in Media Communication* 30.2 (2013): 135–51. Web.

Gossman, Lionel. "Anecdote and History." *History and Theory* 42.2 (2003): 143–68. Web.

Gray, Mary L. *Out in the Country: Youth, Media, and Queer Visibility in Rural America.* New York: New York UP, 2009. Print.

Gregg, Ronald. "Queering Brad Pitt: The Struggle between Gay Fans and the Hollywood Machine to Control Star Discourse and Image on the Web." Pullen and Cooper 139–46.

Gross, Larry P. *Up from Invisibility: Lesbians, Gay Men, and the Media in America.* New York: Columbia UP, 2001. Print.

Halberstam, Judith. *In a Queer Time and Place: Transgender Bodies, Subcultural Lives.* New York: New York UP, 2005. Print.

———. *Female Masculinity.* Durham, NC: Duke UP, 1998. Print.

———. *The Queer Art of Failure.* Durham, NC: Duke UP, 2011. Print.

———. "Shame and White Gay Masculinity." *Social Text* 23 (2005): 219–33. Web.

Hall, Radclyffe. *The Well of Loneliness.* Ed. Havelock Ellis. New York: Covici Friede, 1929. Print.

Halperin, David M. *How to Do the History of Homosexuality.* Chicago: U of Chicago, 2002. Print.

Hammer, Barbara. *Hammer! Making Movies out of Sex and Life.* New York: Feminist, 2010. Print.

———. "Special Feature." *History Lessons.* Prod. Barbara Hammer. Dir. Barbara Hammer. Barbara Hammer, 2000. DVD.

Handelman, Michelle, and Barbara Hammer. "Interview: Barbara Hammer Teaches (and Titillates with) 'History Lessons.'" *Indiewire Movie News.* N.p., 25 Oct. 2001. Web. 9 May 2013.

Hartman, Saidiya. "Venus in Two Acts." *Small Axe: A Caribbean Journal of Criticism* 12.2 (2008): 1–14. Print.

Hemmings, Clare. "From Lesbian Nation to Transgender Liberation: A Bisexual Feminist Perspective." *Journal of Gay, Lesbian and Bisexual Identity* 1.1 (1996): 37–60. Print.

Hilderbrand, Lucas. "Retroactivism." *GLQ: A Journal of Lesbian and Gay Studies* 12.2 (2006): 303–17. Web.

History Lessons. Prod. Barbara Hammer. Dir. Barbara Hammer. Barbara Hammer, 2000. DVD.

Howard, John. *Men Like That: A Southern Queer History.* Chicago: U of Chicago P, 1999. Print.

Hutcheon, Linda. *The Politics of Postmodernism.* London: Routledge, 1989. Print.

Jagose, Annamarie. *Inconsequence: Lesbian Representation and the Logic of Sexual Sequence*. Ithaca: Cornell UP, 2002. Print.

———. "The Trouble with Antinormativity." *Differences* 26.1 (2015): 26–47. Web.

Jarratt, Susan. "Speaking to the Past: Feminist Historiography in Rhetoric." *Pre-Text: A Journal of Rhetorical Theory* 11.3–4 (1990): 189–209. Web.

Jensen, Kyle. "Mythic Transformations: Kenneth Burke Meets the Writing Cow." Rhetoric Society of America Conference. Atlanta, GA. 29 May 2016. Lecture.

Jensen, Kyle, and Krista Ratcliffe. "Mythic Historiography: Refiguring Kenneth Burke's Deceitful Woman Trope." *Rhetoric Society Quarterly* 47 (2017): 1-20. Web.

Juhasz, Alexandra. *Women of Vision: Histories in Feminist Film and Video*. Minneapolis: U of Minnesota P, 2001. Print.

Kaelynandlucy. "About." *YouTube*. Web. https://www.youtube.com/user/kaelynandlucy/about. Accessed 18 July 2017.

———. "Lucy: My Coming Out Story." *YouTube*. 3 July 2012. Web. 12 Nov. 2016.

Kalcik, Susan. "'. . . Like Ann's Gynecologist or the Time I Was Almost Raped': Personal Narratives in Women's Rap Groups." *Journal of American Folklore* 88.347 (1975): 3–11. Web.

Kirsch, Gesa, and Liz Rohan. *Beyond the Archives: Research as a Lived Process*. Carbondale: Southern Illinois UP, 2008. Print.

Kress, Gunther R. *Multimodality: A Social Semiotic Approach to Contemporary Communication*. London: Routledge, 2010. Print.

The Ladder. New York: Arno, 1975. Print.

Lazzara, Damon Lindler. "YouTube Courtship: The Private Ins and Public Outs of Chris and Nickas." Pullen and Cooper 51–61.

Leonard, Zoe, and Cheryl Dunye. *The Fae Richards Photo Archive*. San Francisco: Artspace, 1996. Print.

"The Lesbian Herstory Archives: Virtual Tour." Lesbian Herstory Archives. Web. 12 Nov. 2016.

The Lesbian Herstory Archives Newsletter. Lesbian Herstory Archives, 1975–2004. Print.

LHA Newsletter. See *The Lesbian Herstory Archives Newsletter*.

Logan, Shirley W. *With Pen and Voice: A Critical Anthology of Nineteenth-Century African-American Women*. Carbondale: Southern Illinois UP, 1995. Print.

Louÿs, Pierre. *The Songs of Bilitis*. Trans. Alvah Cecil Bessie. New York: Dover Publications, 1988. Print.

Love, Heather. *Feeling Backward: Loss and the Politics of Queer History*. Cambridge, MA: Harvard UP, 2007. Print.

Lowenthal, David. *The Past Is a Foreign Country.* Cambridge: Cambridge UP, 1985. Print.

Lunsford, Andrea A. *Reclaiming Rhetorica: Women in the Rhetorical Tradition.* Pittsburgh: U of Pittsburgh, 1995. Print.

MacCulloch, Bunny. Interview. *Lesbian News* 12.1 (1986).

MacCulloch (Bunny) Papers. The June L. Mazer Archives at UCLA Special Collections.

Majkowski, Tina. "The 'It Gets Better Campaign': An Unfortunate Use of Queer Futurity." *Women and Performance: A Journal of Feminist Theory* 21.1 (2011): 163–65. Web.

Making Invisible Histories Visible: A Resource Guide to Collections; The June L Mazer Archives. Ed. Kathleen A. McHugh, Brenda Johnson-Grau, and Ben Raphael Sher. Los Angeles: UCLA Center for the Study of Women, 2014.

Manovich, Lev. *The Language of New Media.* Cambridge, MA: MIT P, 2002. Print.

Martin, Del, and Phyllis Lyon. *Lesbian/Woman.* San Francisco: Glide Publications, 1972. Print.

Mattingly, Carol. "Telling Evidence: Rethinking What Counts in Rhetoric." *Rhetoric Society Quarterly* 32.1 (2002): 99–108. Print.

Mazer (June) Papers. June L. Mazer Archives at UCLA Special Collections.

Mazerarchives. "June L. Mazer Archives Serving the Community for 32 Years!" *YouTube.* Web. 13 Mar. 2015.

Mbembe, Achille. "The Power of the Archive and Its Limits." *Refiguring the Archive.* Ed. Carolyn Hamilton. Cape Town, South Africa: David Philip, 2002. 19–28. Print.

McBean, Sam. "Remediating Affect: 'Luclyn' and Lesbian Intimacy on YouTube." *Journal of Lesbian Studies* 18.3 (2014): 282–97. Web.

McCalls Publishing Correspondence, 1970–71. Writings, Phyllis Lyon and Del Martin Papers, 93-13, Gay, Lesbian, Bisexual, Transgender Historical Society, San Francisco.

McLellan, Diana. *The Girls: Sappho Goes to Hollywood.* New York: LA Weekly, 2000. Print.

Meeker, Martin. *Contacts Desired: Gay and Lesbian Communications and Community, 1940s–1970s.* Chicago: U of Chicago, 2006. Print.

Miller, Carolyn R. "The Aristotelian Topos: Hunting for Novelty." *Rereading Aristotle's Rhetoric.* Ed. Alan G. Gross and Arthur E. Walzer. Carbondale: Southern Illinois UP, 2000. 130–46. Print.

———. "Foreword." Selber, *Rhetorics*, ix–xii. Print.

Miller, Neil. *Out of the Past: Gay and Lesbian History from 1869 to the Present.* New York: Vintage, 1995. Print.

Milton, John. *Samson Agonistes*. London: Oxford UP, 1957. Print.

Morris, Charles E. "Archival Queer." *Rhetoric and Public Affairs* 9.1 (2006): 145–51. Print.

———. "The Archival Turn in Rhetorical Studies; or, The Archive's Rhetorical (Re)turn." *Rhetoric and Public Affairs* 9.1 (2006): 113–15. Print.

Morris, Charles E., ed. *Queering Public Address: Sexualities in American Historical Discourse*. Columbia: U of South Carolina P, 2007. Print.

Morris, Charles E., and K. J. Rawson. "Queer Archives/Archival Queers." Ballif, *Theorizing* 74–89.

Muñoz, José Esteban. *Cruising Utopia: The Then and There of Queer Futurity*. New York: New York UP, 2009. Print.

———. *Disidentifications: Queers of Color and the Performance of Politics*. Minneapolis: U of Minnesota P, 1999. Print.

———. "Ephemera as Evidence: Introductory Notes to Queer Acts." *Women and Performance: A Journal of Feminist Theory* 8.2 (1996): 5–16. Print.

Murray, Joddy. *Non-discursive Rhetoric: Image and Affect in Multimodal Composition*. Albany: SUNY P, 2009. Print.

Nealon, Christopher. *Foundlings: Lesbian and Gay Historical Emotion before Stonewall*. Durham, NC: Duke UP, 2001. Print.

Nestle, Joan. Correspondence with the author. July 2011. E-mail.

———. "Notes on Radical Archiving from a Lesbian Feminist Standpoint." *Gay Insurgent* 4.5 (1979): 10–11. Print.

———. "Who Were We to Do Such a Thing? Grassroots Necessities, Grassroots Dreaming." *Radical History Review* 2015.122 (2015): 233–42. Web.

———. "The Will to Remember: The Lesbian Herstory Archives of New York." *Feminist Review* 34.1 (1990): 86–94. Print.

———. "The Will to Remember: The Lesbian Herstory Archives of New York." *Journal of Homosexuality* 34:3-4 (1998): 225–35.

Nitrate Kisses. Dir. Barbara Hammer. Barbara Hammer, 1992. DVD.

No Secret Anymore: The Times of Del Martin and Phyllis Lyon. Dir. Joan E. Biren. Frameline, 2003. DVD.

Noble, Greg. "Accumulating Being." *International Journal of Cultural Studies* 7.2 (2004): 233–56. Print.

Not Just Passing Through. Dir. Jean Carlomusto, Dolores Perez, Catherine Gund Saalfield, and Polly Thistlewaite. Women Make Movies, 1994. DVD.

Olson, Hope. "Difference, Culture, and Change: The Untapped Potential of LCSH." *Cataloging and Classification Quarterly* 29.1–2 (2000): 53–71. Print.

Organization Files. Lesbian Herstory Archives.

O'Riordan, Kate. "Queer Theories and Cybersubjects: Intersecting Figures." *Queer Online Media Technology and Sexuality*. New York: Lang, 2007. Print.

Phelan, Peggy. "The Serious Comedy of Hope: Introducing the Five Lesbian Brothers." *Five Lesbian Brothers, Four Plays*. New York: Theatre Communications Group, 2000. Xiii-xix. Print.

Phillips, Laurie M. "Offering Hope and Making Attributions through YouTube: An Exploratory Ethnographic Content Analysis of the Social Change–Oriented 'It Gets Better Project.'" *Journal of Social Media in Society* 2.1 (Spring 2013): 30–65. Web.

Piontek, Thomas. *Queering Gay and Lesbian Studies*. Urbana: U of Illinois P, 2006. Print.

Plato. *Phaedrus*. Ed. Harvey Yunis. Cambridge: Cambridge UP, 2011. Print.

Pullen, Christopher, and Margaret Cooper, eds. *LGBT Identity and Online New Media*. New York: Routledge, 2010. Print.

Ramos, Jaunita, ed. *Compañeras: Latina Lesbians; An Anthology*. New York: Latina Lesbian History Project, 1987. Print.

Ratcliffe, Krista. "'Hey There, Delilah': Refiguring Our Identifications with Burke's Deceitful Woman Trope." Rhetoric Society of America Conference. Atlanta, GA. 29 May 2016. Lecture.

Rawson, K. J. "Accessing Transgender // Desiring Queer(er?) Archival Logics." *Archivaria* 68 (2009): 123–140. Web.

———. "Archiving Transgender: Affects, Logics, and the Power of Queer History." Diss. Syracuse University. Thesis/Dissertation ETD, 2010. Web.

———. "Queering Feminist Rhetorical Canonization." *Rhetorica in Motion: Feminist Rhetorical Methods and Methodologies*. Ed. Eileen E. Schell and K. J. Rawson. Pittsburgh: U of Pittsburgh P, 2010. 39–52. Print.

Reid-Pharr, Robert F. "Makes Me Feel Mighty Real: *The Watermelon Woman* and the Critique of Black Visuality." *F Is for Phony: Fake Documentary and Truth's Undoing*. Ed. Alexandra Juhasz and Jesse Lerner. Minneapolis: U of Minnesota P, 2006. 130–42.

Rice, Jeff. *The Rhetoric of Cool: Composition Studies and New Media*. Carbondale: Southern Illinois UP, 2007. Print.

Rich, B. Ruby. "New Queer Cinema." *New Queer Cinema: A Critical Reader*. Ed. Michele Aaron. New Brunswick, NJ: Rutgers UP, 2004. 15–22. Print.

Robertson, Pamela. "What Makes the Feminist Camp?" Cleto, *Camp* 266–82.

Rody, Caroline. "Toni Morrison's *Beloved*: History, 'Rememory,' and a 'Clamor for a Kiss.'" *American Literary History* 7.1 (1995): 92–119. Web. 12 Nov. 2016.

Rohy, Valerie. "In the Queer Archive: *Fun Home*." *GLQ: A Journal of Lesbian and Gay Studies* 16.3 (2010): 341–61. Web.

Royster, Jacqueline Jones. *Traces of a Stream: Literacy and Social Change among African American Women*. Pittsburgh: U of Pittsburgh P, 2000. Print.

Schwarz, Judith. "Researching Lesbian History." *Sinister Wisdom* 5 (1978): 55–59. Web.

Scott, Joan W. "The Evidence of Experience." *Critical Inquiry* 17.4 (1991): 773–97. Print.

Sedgwick, Eve Kosofsky. *Between Men: English Literature and Male Homosocial Desire.* New York: Columbia UP, 1985. Print.

Selber, Stuart A. "Introduction." Selber, *Rhetorics.* Print.

———, ed. *Rhetorics and Technologies: New Directions in Writing and Communication.* Columbia: U of South Carolina P, 2010. Print.

Sharer, Wendy. "Disintegrating Bodies of Knowledge: Historical Material and Revisionary Histories of Rhetoric." *Rhetorical Bodies.* Ed. Jack Selzer and Sharon Crowley. Madison: U of Wisconsin P, 1999. 120–42. Print.

Sher, Ben Raphael. "Mysteries of the June L. Mazer Lesbian Archives: Martha Foster Collection." *Newsletter for the UCLA Center for the Study of Women*, Fall 2013, 19–21. Web.

Sheridan, David M., Jim Ridolfo, and Anthony J. Michel. "The Available Means of Persuasion: Mapping a Theory and Pedagogy of Multimodal Public Rhetoric." *JAC:* 25.4 (2005): 803–44. Web.

Signorile, Michelangelo. "The Secret Gay Life of Malcolm Forbes." *Outweek* (New York), 18 March 1990. Print.

A Simple Matter of Justice: The 1993 March on Washington for Lesbian, Gay, and Bi Equal Rights and Representation. Dir. Joan E. Biren. Frameline, 1993. DVD.

Smith, Ralph, and Russell Windes. "Civil Rights Movements and Queer Identities: Complexities of the Collective Subject." Morris, *Queering* 45–73. *Queering Public Address: Sexualities in American Historical Discourse.* Ed. Charles E. Morris. Columbia, SC: U of South Carolina, 2007. 45–73. Print.

Starn, Randolph. "Historicizing: A Formal Exercise." *Representations* 104.1 (2008): 137–43. Print.

Stoler, Ann L. "Colonial Archives and the Arts of Governance: On the Content in the Form." *Refiguring the Archive.* Ed. Carolyn Hamilton. Cape Town, South Africa: David Philip, 2002. 83–100. Print.

Streitmatter, Rodger. *Empty without You: The Intimate Letters of Eleanor Roosevelt and Lorena Hickok.* New York: Free, 2000. Print.

Subject Files. Lesbian Herstory Archives.

Taylor, Verta, and Nancy Whittier. "Collective Identity in Social Movement Communities: Lesbian Feminist Mobilization." *Waves of Protest.* Ed. Jo Freeman and Victoria Johnson. Lanham, MD: Rowman and Littlefield Publishers, 1999. Print.

Tender Fictions. Prod. Barbara Hammer. Dir. Barbara Hammer. Barbara Hammer, 1996. DVD.

Thistlewaite, Polly J. "Building 'A Home of Our Own': The Construction of the Lesbian Herstory Archives." Carmichael 153–74.

———. "The Lesbian and Gay Past: An Interpretive Battleground." *Gay Community News* (New York), Feb. 1995. Print.

Velody, Irving. "The Archive and the Human Sciences: Notes towards a Theory of the Archive." *History of the Human Sciences* 11.4 (1998): 1–16. Print.

Vicinus, Martha. "'They Wonder to Which Sex I Belong': The Historical Roots of the Modern Lesbian Identity." *Feminist Studies* 18.3 (Lesbian Issue; 1992): 467–97. *JSTOR*. Web. 17 Jan. 2015.

Warner, Michael. "Introduction." *Fear of a Queer Planet: Queer Politics and Social Theory*. Minneapolis: U of Minnesota P, 1993. vii–xxxi. Print.

———. "Publics and Counterpublics." *Public Culture* 14.1 (2002): 49–90. Print.

The Watermelon Woman. Dir. Cheryl Dunye. First Run Features, 1997. DVD.

Wells, Susan. "Technology, Genre, and Gender: The Case of Power Structure Research." Selber, *Rhetorics*. Print.

"What Is the It Gets Better Project?" *It Gets Better Project*. 2010. Web. http://www.itgetsbetter.org/pages/about-it-gets-better-project/. Accessed August 2014.

White, Hayden V. *The Practical Past*. Evanston, IL: Northwestern UP, 2014. Print.

Williams, Raymond. *The Long Revolution*. New York: Columbia UP, 1961. Print.

Wolf, Steve. "Sex and the Single Cataloger." *Revolting Librarians*. Ed. Celeste West and Elizabeth Katz. San Francisco: Booklegger, 1972. Print.

"WOW Cafe Theatre." *WOW Cafe Theatre*. Web. 9 May 2013.

INDEX

Page locators in italics refer to figures.

Jean Bessette is an assistant professor at the University of Vermont, where she teaches rhetoric and writing courses that address issues in gender and sexuality, historiography, and multimodality. Her work has appeared in *Rhetoric Review*, *College Composition and Communication*, *Rhetoric Society Quarterly*, and *Computers and Composition*.

Studies in Rhetorics and Feminisms

Studies in Rhetorics and Feminisms seeks to address the interdisciplinarity that rhetorics and feminisms represent. Rhetorical and feminist scholars want to connect rhetorical inquiry with contemporary academic and social concerns, exploring rhetoric's relevance to current issues of opportunity and diversity. This interdisciplinarity has already begun to transform the rhetorical tradition as we have known it (upper-class, agonistic, public, and male) into regendered, inclusionary rhetorics (democratic, dialogic, collaborative, cultural, and private). Our intellectual advancements depend on such ongoing transformation.

Rhetoric, whether ancient, contemporary, or futuristic, always inscribes the relation of language and power at a particular moment, indicating who may speak, who may listen, and what can be said. The only way we can displace the traditional rhetoric of masculine-only, public performance is to replace it with rhetorics that are recognized as being better suited to our present needs. We must understand more fully the rhetorics of the non-Western tradition, of women, of a variety of cultural and ethnic groups. Therefore, Studies in Rhetorics and Feminisms espouses a theoretical position of openness and expansion, a place for rhetorics to grow and thrive in a symbiotic relationship with all that feminisms have to offer, particularly when these two fields intersect with philosophical, sociological, religious, psychological, pedagogical, and literary issues.

The series seeks scholarly works that both examine and extend rhetoric, works that span the sexes, disciplines, cultures, ethnicities, and sociocultural practices as they intersect with the rhetorical tradition. After all, the recent resurgence of rhetorical studies has been not so much a discovery of new rhetorics as a recognition of existing rhetorical activities and practices, of our newfound ability and willingness to listen to previously untold stories.

The series editors seek both high-quality traditional and cutting-edge scholarly work that extends the significant relationship between rhetoric and feminism within various genres, cultural contexts, historical periods, methodologies, theoretical positions, and methods of delivery (e.g., film and hypertext to elocution and preaching).

Queries and submissions:
Professor Cheryl Glenn, Editor
E-mail: cjg6@psu.edu

Professor Shirley Wilson Logan, Editor
E-mail: slogan@umd.edu

Studies in Rhetorics and Feminisms
Department of English
142 South Burrowes Bldg.

Penn State University
University Park, PA 16802-6200

Other Books in the Studies in Rhetorics and Feminisms Series

Feminist Rhetorical Science Studies: Human Bodies, Posthumanist Worlds
Edited by Amanda K. Booher and Julie Jung

A Feminist Legacy: The Rhetoric and Pedagogy of Gertrude Buck
Suzanne Bordelon

Regendering Delivery: The Fifth Canon and Antebellum Women Rhetors
Lindal Buchanan

Rhetorics of Motherhood
Lindal Buchanan

Conversational Rhetoric: The Rise and Fall of a Women's Tradition, 1600–1900
Jane Donawerth

Feminism beyond Modernism
Elizabeth A. Flynn

Women and Rhetoric between the Wars
Edited by Ann George, M. Elizabeth Weiser, and Janet Zepernick

Educating the New Southern Woman: Speech, Writing, and Race at the Public Women's Colleges, 1884–1945
David Gold and Catherine L. Hobbs

Food, Feminisms, Rhetorics
Edited by Melissa A. Goldthwaite

Women's Irony: Rewriting Feminist Rhetorical Histories
Tarez Samra Graban

Claiming the Bicycle: Women, Rhetoric, and Technology in Nineteenth-Century America
Sarah Hallenbeck

The Rhetoric of Rebel Women: Civil War Diaries and Confederate Persuasion
Kimberly Harrison

Evolutionary Rhetoric: Sex, Science, and Free Love in Nineteenth-Century Feminism
Wendy Hayden

Liberating Voices: Writing at the Bryn Mawr Summer School for Women Workers
Karyn L. Hollis

Gender and Rhetorical Space in American Life, 1866–1910
Nan Johnson

Antebellum American Women's Poetry: A Rhetoric of Sentiment
Wendy Dasler Johnson

Appropriate[ing] Dress: Women's Rhetorical Style in Nineteenth-Century America
Carol Mattingly

The Gendered Pulpit: Preaching in American Protestant Spaces
Roxanne Mountford

Writing Childbirth: Women's Rhetorical Agency in Labor and Online
Kim Hensley Owens

Rhetorical Listening: Identification, Gender, Whiteness
Krista Ratcliffe

Feminist Rhetorical Practices: New Horizons for Rhetoric, Composition, and Literacy Studies
Jacqueline J. Royster and Gesa E. Kirsch

Rethinking Etho: A Feminist Ecological Approach to Rhetoric
Edited by Kathleen J. Ryan, Nancy Myers, and Rebecca Jones

Vote and Voice: Women's Organizations and Political Literacy, 1915–1930
Wendy B. Sharer

Women Physicians and Professional Ethos in Nineteenth-Century America
Carolyn Skinner

Praising Girls: The Rhetoric of Young Women, 1895–1930
Henrietta Rix Wood